Atomic Soldiers

ATOMIC SOLDIERS

American Victims of Nuclear Experiments

Howard L. Rosenberg

Beacon Press
Boston

Copyright © 1980 by Howard L. Rosenberg
Beacon Press books are published under the auspices
of the Unitarian Universalist Association
Published simultaneously in Canada by
Fitzhenry & Whiteside Limited, Toronto

(hardcover) 9 8 7 6 5 4 3 2 1

Library of Congress Cataloging in Publication Data
Rosenberg, Howard L 1951–
   Atomic soldiers.
   Bibliography: p.
   Includes index.
   1.   Veterans—diseases—United States.   2.   Atomic
   Bomb—Physiological effects.   3.   Radiation—Toxi-
   cology.   4.   Atomic weapons—Testing.   I   Title.
UB369.R67   1980   355'.0217   79-3781
ISBN 0-8070-3210-7

For Katie Rose

ACKNOWLEDGMENTS

Gathering the information for the writing of this book was like trying to complete a jigsaw puzzle without all the pieces. I owe a large debt of gratitude to a number of people who furnished clues to the location of some of the pieces and provided temporary haven for the author, as well as inspiration and production and editing help with the manuscript. Though I can't thank all the librarians, records clerks and secretaries, some deserve special mention.

Several government officials were very helpful in providing crucial data, and many were quite gracious about sharing time with me. Among them, special thanks go to Mahlon "Ink" Gates, Dave Jackson and Dave Miller of the U.S. Department of Energy's Nevada Operations Office. I'd also like to thank Cliff Penwell of the Reynolds Electrical and Engineering Company for proving to be a sure-footed and knowledgeable guide on the desert.

Hank Greenspun, Brian Greenspun and Jeff Adler of the Las Vegas *Sun* were generous both with their time and the newspaper's facilities.

In Washington, I offer my appreciation to congressional staffers Walter Sheridan, Patrick McLain and Molly Mulligan and to the Defense Nuclear Agency's Vice Admiral Robert Monroe and Lieutenant Colonel Bill McGee for their cooperation. Doctor Saul Lavisky of the Human Resources Research Organization was a great help in locating former members of the firm and providing data on HumRRO's work during the atmospheric bomb tests.

During my travels while researching this book, Ralph and Sara Denton and Russell, Marjorie and Leona Dann went to extraordinary lengths to insure that my stays in Nevada and Minnesota were both enjoyable and productive. For their hospitality, I shall always be grateful.

To Robert Alvarez, thanks for encouraging me to write about the atomic soldiers in the first place, and to my editor, Tom Walter, thanks for the help and support he showed throughout the project. The suggestions of Les Whitten, Robert Russell and Opal Ginn were a boon at critical points, and to my parents and John Joseph Francis Keenan in Omaha, Nebraska, I owe a word of thanks for their inspiration and confidence many years ago.

To Paula Humbert, I'm much obliged for her typing and proofreading skills, and to my dear wife, Kathleen, I will forever be indebted for her tireless efforts in typing and retyping my manuscript, proofreading and the remarkable patience she exhibited and the heartening words she offered when her wise and cheerful counsel was sorely needed.

PREFACE

Often, during the course of researching and writing this book, I was asked whether it was fair to make moral judgments on events that took place twenty years ago.

My reply then, and now, is the same. No, it is not fair for me to make moral judgments, and I have carefully avoided them. It was never my intention to hold the purveyors of past national policy up to a judge's bar. Rather, my aim all along was to strip away the cloak of secrecy that surrounded the atomic testing program and allow those events to be viewed in a clear light, without the shadings of bogus claims of national security or the blotted ink of a censor's stamp.

I have endeavored to tell the story of the atomic soldiers in the context of the temper of the times and have re-created some conversations between them after extensive interviews. Other conversations are verbatim quotes from the participants, or are directly quoted from heretofore secret Pentagon reports, and meeting transcripts, memoranda, and letters of the Atomic Energy Commission.

I hope that by reviewing the political climate in which decisions were made to expose hundreds of thousands of American servicemen and civilians to the vagaries of atom bomb explosions, the reader will be able to make the judgment I have avoided. Indeed, it is a judgment that must be made if Americans are to decide once and for all whether the benefits to be gained from letting the nuclear genie out of the bottle are worth the high price it may cost in lives.

In a very real sense, we are all "atomic soldiers," destined to be the guinea pigs for an ongoing scientific experiment. If the fears of an ever-growing number of scientists are indeed well founded, then the nation's headlong rush into the nuclear age will eventually take its toll in dramatic increases of fatal cancers among the populace. When, and if, that occurs, a rush to judgment will, ironically, be too late.

All of the critical issues of nuclear weapons and nuclear power development have their roots in the atomic tests in Nevada during the 1950s: the effects of fallout, the relationship between low-level radiation exposure and cancer, the elitism that allowed a few men to make decisions that affect us all, the legal precedents surrounding government culpability and the moral questions of whether the cost can be justified.

The issues can be examined in microcosm, reflected in the story of one man — Russell Jack Dann, a corporal with the 82nd Airborne Division and a subject of psychological experiments in the Nevada desert during the summer of 1957. In many ways, the naive, patriotic Corporal Dann was Everyman in the United States, lulled into a false sense of security by the soothing assurances of policymakers that they had everything under control and that his safety was foremost in their thoughts. What happened to Corporal Dann has happened to us all. Today, like him, we are a bit wiser and a lot more skeptical. To ignore the story of the atomic soldiers would be to ignore a dramatic tragedy of today and a warning for tomorrow.

The first casualty of the atomic testing program was the truth. And then came the soldiers. It is to those casualties that this book is dedicated.

Howard L. Rosenberg
Silver Spring, Maryland
January 1980

CONTENTS

INTRODUCTION

by JACK ANDERSON

On August 6, 1945 — the dreadful day that the atomic genie was let out of the bottle and the first towering mushroom cloud rose over Hiroshima — mankind held its breath for an awful moment. Then the cheering began.

There was cheering in Washington because the Americans had beaten the Nazis in the deadly race to develop the ultimate weapon. When it was learned that two German physicists had discovered the formula for nuclear fission, American scientists recognized this as the key to a weapon that would win the war. They had alerted U.S. leaders who had committed all the nation's resources to the race. Thousands of dedicated scientists, patriotic bureaucrats and skilled workmen had labored night and day to perfect the first atomic bomb.

There was cheering across America, which had been braced for a bloody invasion of the Japanese islands. American troops had faced the foreboding prospect of waging a prolonged city-by-city, house-by-house conquest of a fanatical enemy. Then Hiroshima was obliterated by a single blast. Three days later, Nagasaki was destroyed and the Japanese swiftly surrendered. Hundreds of thousands of American lives were saved by ending the war without the need for an allied invasion.

There was cheering in the backwaters of China where I had been wandering about the interior with a Nationalist guerrilla group, riding its one horse. As a young, unsung war correspondent, I had managed to cover only one skirmish, not against the Japanese enemy, to be sure, but rather against a Chinese Communist unit. The news of Hiroshima and Nagasaki reached us through the crackling and wheezing of a primitive radio powered by a hand-cranked generator. Then one of the guerrillas, a slight, unforgettable fellow named King Junshang, rushed up to me and blurted: "Japs surrendered! Japs surrendered!"

But not everyone was cheering. The man who was soon to become my employer, Drew Pearson, had deep misgivings about the awesome new weapon. Even as the second bomb was pulverizing Nagasaki, Drew warned soberly that the "danger of the bomb to future civilization is

1

almost beyond belief, once the secret becomes known." And this, he predicted, would be merely a matter of time. "An invention of this kind," he wrote, "is sure to leak out just as every military weapon sooner or later becomes known."

The federal custodians of the terrible secret responded to the danger with a strange schizophrenia. On the one hand, they began protecting their secret with a quiet, almost paranoid panic. They tried by edict to cram the genie back in the bottle. They banned all discussion and speculation about the atomic bomb. The censorship directive covered everything from the bomb's workings and postwar usage to international agreements and possible medical applications.

They adopted the attitude that only they could be trusted with their Frankenstein's plaything, that only they really understood its horror and possessed the moral fiber to protect civilization. They became suspicious even of the scientists who had developed the bomb. This presented an awkward dilemma: how could the federal guardians withhold the atomic secret from the scientists who had created it? The attempt was made, nonetheless, using oppressive security regulations and witch hunts.

On the other hand, the builders of the bomb wound up after World War II with a vast nuclear-industrial complex and no more enemy cities to disintegrate. It is not the nature of a bureaucracy to disband after its work is completed; rather, the bureaucrats become entrenched in the granite and sandstone compounds of government.

So the heroes of the Manhattan Project, who had pushed and labored and sacrificed so hard to gain nuclear supremacy for the United States, began to behave in peacetime like normal, routine-bound bureaucrats — some by dozing at their desks, some by becoming the world's most methodical readers of newspapers, others by making empires out of molehills, still others by developing a mastery of the regulation books in order to confound the real world.

To justify their continuing existence, they switched from wartime to peacetime goals without missing a turn of a mimeograph machine. They designed nuclear reactors as a source of cheap power. So eager were they to attain this golden nuclear age — and, in the process, to perpetuate their jobs and preserve their bureaucratic fiefdoms — that they began sharing their nuclear technology with a waiting, wondering world.

It is quite impossible, of course, to share peaceful nuclear knowledge and, at the same time, withold military nuclear secrets, for the reactor and the bomb are fruit of the same tree. This obvious contradiction did not deter our federal decision-makers from pursuing both policies at once; they taught foreign nations some of the same secrets that they vigilantly safeguarded.

If the official policies were illogical, the enforcement was irrational and the results inevitable. While nuclear scientists from abroad trained in the United States, grim security men hounded the American scientists who had fathered the atomic bomb. One after another, these distinguished scientists were put through federal inquisitions.

Dr. J. Robert Oppenheimer, whose Los Alamos laboratory was the birthplace of the bomb, was subjected to shabby investigations and indignities. In the end, he was hounded out of government — his brilliant, inventive brain no longer available to this country. Bernard Peters, a naturalized American citizen who had escaped Nazi Germany, joined the atomic project and put his genius to work for his adopted country. But because of some obscure political associations, he also lost his government clearance. David Bohm, one of the world's leading authorities on thermonuclear gases, received the same treatment. Sadly, he imigrated to Israel.

In fact, most of the atomic pioneers, having associated with the ostracized scientists, became suspect, for guilt-by-association ruled the day. They were given minimal initiative and were no longer trusted with sensitive information. Of course, scientists who are denied trust and blocked from access to information seldom produce great discoveries, and a nation that inhibits the free exchange of ideas must risk the possibility that its thinkers will journey elsewhere.

But government regulations notwithstanding, it is nigh onto impossible to stifle ideas. Information cannot be dammed up behind national borders for long. Relatively few facts must really be kept secret, therefore, to protect national security. More likely, government officials will use the secrecy stamp to protect themselves. For in their heart of hearts, they are at odds with democracy. They abhor conflict that disrupts the smooth implementation of their plans and procedures; they embrace secrecy because what is not known cannot be disrupted.

Thus most nuclear officials, following their natural disposition, tried to sweep their mistakes and miscalculations under the secrecy stamp. The public was not supposed to be told about the nuclear wastes, radioactive seepages and reactor malfunctions that marred the official ideal of a Nuclear Utopia.

To this day, the American people remain in official darkness about the lethal fallout from the atomic-bomb tests of the 1950s. Disquieting questions were raised about atmospheric testing, and disturbing consequences were chronicled. But these were summarily suppressed.

From its inception at Los Alamos to the near miss at Three Mile Island, the history of nuclear power has been plagued with too much haste, which has created incalculable dangers, and overzealous secrecy, which has concealed the truth from the endangered populace. Howard Rosenberg has covered this awesome story for me. His book *Atomic Soldiers* marshals the frightening facts he has gathered. It tells of bomb tests that produced a fallout of government lies and deceit. I hope its revelations will stir the American conscience.

PROLOGUE

FORT BRAGG, NORTH CAROLINA
AUGUST 1957

Corporal Russell Jack Dann felt an uneasiness rumble up from the pit of his stomach as he settled back into a canvas sling along the plane's bulkhead and waited quietly for the pilots to lift C–124 Globemaster's lumbering body skyward. It wasn't the usual anxiety that all paratroopers feel before a jump that had the 20-year-old soldier's guts tied in knots but rather the uncertainty of what to expect when he finally faced the atomic bomb he knew was waiting for him on a desolate strip of Nevada desert.

As he added up all the things that didn't seem quite right about this mission, Dann began to wonder if perhaps he had made a mistake by volunteering so quickly. Already a veteran of more than 24 jumps, the corporal was discomforted by the thought that, for the first time in his 30-month Army career, he was on a plane without a parachute strapped to his back. The fact that he was asked to fill out a next-of-kin notification before boarding the plane didn't do much to set his mind at ease either.

The roar of the Globemaster's four engines drowned out the chatter in the cabin as the plane taxied along the tarmac and Dann was left to mull over the events of the past few days which had led him to his present set of circumstances.

"You want to go to Camp Desert Rock?" the company clerk asked, stepping through the door of the communications shack where Dann was monotonously inventorying his unit's supply of wire after a recent field exercise.

"Sure," Dann laughed as he turned from the racks of reels. "As long as the booze is free, the women are easy and they ain't got no damned wire to keep track of."

"I'm serious," the clerk said, eyeing Dann disdainfully. "Cap'n says we need two 'volunteer' noncoms with security clearances for a mission to Camp Desert Rock. It's way the hell out in Nevada somewheres. And the captain says you can be spared."

5

"Whadaya mean, I can be spared? I thought I was essential to the smooth operation of this company!"

"Aw, Dann. Quit giving me a hard time. You got three wiremen and an assistant. Any of them guys can do your job. Probably better too. The only noncoms in the company with clearance are you, me, the first sergeant, the supply sergeant, and his assistant, Swanson. So it looks like you and Swanson. Now, do you want to go? I gotta tell Captain Hill."

"How long will I be gone?" Dann asked.

"Only a few days."

"What are we going to do out there?"

"Ask Captain Hill. You wanna go?"

"You betcha. Anything to get out of this como [communications] shack."

"Great. Come on across the hall and talk to the captain."

Dann hooked his clipboard on a nail next to the door jamb and tucked his fatigue shirt tightly into the waistband of his trousers. He lifted first one foot and then the other, rubbing the toes of his spit-shined jump boots on the back of his trousers to wipe off the thin layer of dust that had settled on them. Donning his cap, Dann crossed the corridor into the orderly room, nodded at the scowling first sergeant and rapped loudly on the captain's door.

"Enter!" thundered a voice that was only slightly muffled by the door. Dann twisted the door knob and walked briskly across the threshold. He slammed the door behind him, swept his cap off with his left hand and saluted smartly with his right toward the broad-shouldered black man sitting behind the desk.

"Corporal Dann reporting as ordered, sir!" Dann said, raising his voice at the end of the phrase so it was more a bellow than a statement.

"Dann, can't you enter my office without slamming the door?"

"Yes, sir!" Dann shouted again. He tried to be as formal and polite as possible with Captain Hill. He knew the officer didn't like him and the feeling was mutual. But Dann figured that by being the "perfect soldier" to an extreme, he could get under the captain's skin without giving the man an excuse to bust him for insubordination.

"Then next time, damnit, just shut the goddamned door. Don't slam it."

"Yes, sir!" said Dann, trying hard to stifle a grin.

"The clerk tells me you want to 'volunteer' for this Camp Desert Rock mission."

"Well, sir," Dann paused. "I'd kind of like to know a bit more about the mission. The clerk didn't tell me too much."

"I don't know too much about it myself. They're putting together a provisional company of troopers to be observers at an atomic shot out there in Nevada and they need a couple of volunteers from each company. It'll only be for a few days and we can get along without you here. Now, are you volunteering or not? I haven't got all day."

Dann could tell the captain was rapidly losing patience with him.

"Will you be going, sir?" Dann asked, hoping that this last question wouldn't send the captain over the edge.

"No, I'm not going. Bill Stovall from the five-o-fourth will be the C.O."

"Well, yes, sir. In that case, then, I volunteer," Dann quickly replied, his face breaking into a grin. The captain looked up at Dann once again with a sneer on his face, and the young corporal judged that the officer was probably glad to be rid of him, if only for a few days.

"O.K. You take off from Pope at 0600 the day after tomorrow. There's a briefing at 0800 tomorrow. Get the details from the clerk."

"Yes, sir!" said Dann, spinning around and reaching for the door knob.

"Oh, corporal!" the captain called after him. "This operation is highly classified, so keep your big mouth shut!"

"Yes, sir!" Dann shouted as he pulled the door behind him and slammed it shut with a jerk.

At the briefing the following morning, the paratroopers answered "Present!" as their names were read from a roster by Captain William Stovall. A sandy-haired man of average height who spoke with a quiet, southern drawl, Stovall was in his late thirties in 1957. That was old for a company commander, but the Lexington, Kentucky, native had the lean, hard looks of a man a decade younger.

An enlisted man during World War II, Stovall was one of the Army Rangers at the Normandy landing who clambered up a steep cliff using ropes and grappling hooks while German machine gunners rained lead on them from above. The Rangers took a foothold on the summit that day, but only after suffering fearsome losses. The deed is still remembered as one of the great feats of wartime derring-do.

After the war, Stovall moved steadily up through the ranks until he was commissioned as a second lieutenant. One of those increasingly rare officers who knew what it was like to be on both sides of the brass, he was highly regarded by his men. Though he spoke softly and eschewed the tough talk common among paratroopers, Stovall had an aura about him that commanded allegiance and respect.

The other six officers assigned to the mission were introduced to the men. Among them were two West Point military academy graduates — First Lieutenant Louis H. Ginn III, a ramrod straight, 24-year-old six-footer with brown hair and the square-jawed look of a soldier that the Army might choose for a recruiting poster, and Second Lieutenant William R. Crites, a debonair officer with an easygoing manner and a ready smile, two years younger than Ginn.

The 163 troopers were divided into two platoons representing the 504th and 505th Airborne Infantry regiments and two platoons made up from the ranks of four airborne field artillery battalions. Dann was assigned to a platoon headed by Lieutenant Ginn. Though there were other corporals in his squad, Ginn made Dann the squad leader because of his seniority.

Some of the men assigned to the mission were the cream of their respective companies. But the majority were there because, like Dann, they were available, had the necessary security clearances or were chosen by default.

Charles "Chuck" Newsome, a 20-year-old corporal from H Company of the 505th, chose himself for the mission. A born hell-raiser from Hampton, Virginia, Newsome was well known at the nearby Fayetteville, North Carolina, jail for his brawling at local bars. He was in trouble so often, his friends joked that Newsome needed zippers on his stripes. The bellicose corporal was also his company's Troop Information and Education noncommissioned officer.

Because of the nature of the job, Newsome was privy to every bit of information that arrived at his unit's orderly room. When the orders came through asking for volunteers, Newsome immediately added his own name to the list.

Gary L. Hamberger didn't have to be asked twice if he wanted to go to Nevada. Under the expert tutelage of his platoon sergeant, Hamberger had been eagerly studying the fine art of craps for months, and the

20-year-old corporal from York, Pennsylvania, was anxious to test his newly learned skill in Las Vegas.

Hamberger was a shy, soft-spoken soldier who avoided the more boisterous antics of barracks life. But with a pair of dice in his palm, Hamberger took on the look of an inveterate gambler, and he always seemed to win.

Robert Schaudenecker was a strapping, six-foot, two-inch, 23-year-old private. A Chicago fireman before he was drafted, Schaudenecker was an adventurous GI who jumped at the opportunity to join the Camp Desert Rock mission.

David L. Icenhour was a 25-year-old medical corpsman from Hickory, North Carolina, who had graduated from noncommissioned officer's school only a few days before the provisional company was formed. The newly anointed sergeant was temporarily unassigned and quickly got the calls for the special assignment.

Captain Stovall explained that the provisional company, designated Task Force Big Bang, was scheduled to participate in atomic "event" number six of the Exercise Desert Rock series then underway in Nevada. Stovall didn't know, or at least he wasn't saying, what the participation entailed. He did caution the soldiers to be on time the next morning because buses to nearby Pope Air Force Base would be departing the headquarters compound promptly at 4:30 A.M. Then the men were dismissed.

"Maybe that's why they call it a briefing," Dann said to the tall, dark-blond-haired sergeant next to him who had also been named to be one of the squad leaders. "They sure don't tell ya much."

"They sure don't," the sergeant shrugged as he offered his hand. "My name's Paul . . . Paul Cooper."

"Nice to meet you, sarge," Dann said, tightly gripping his new friend's outstretched hand. "Mine's Dann. Russell Jack Dann."

"Yeah, I heard Lieutenant Ginn read your name out when we formed up. Are you from the five-o-fourth? I haven't seen you around."

"No. Five-o-fifth over at Old Division. Do you know Lieutenant Ginn?"

"He just transferred into Charlie Company a few weeks ago. Guys in his company tell me he's a West Pointer. He's supposed to be a good man to serve under."

"Great. I'll be glad to get away from my C.O. for a while. He's got it in for me. The son of a bitch ain't nothing but a damn garrison soldier at heart."

"Well, these guys are gonna run our tails off if what I hear about Stovall is true," said Cooper, smiling. Dann could see by the campaign ribbons on the sergeant's "Class A" khaki uniform that he was a Korean War veteran. The young corporal was pleased that he had been named to a position of responsibility equal to troopers the like of Cooper.

"That's all right with me." Dann smiled. "I'm ready to do some real soldiering."

"Well, I have some things to clear up over at my company area," said Cooper. "I'll see you in the morning."

"You betcha, sarge," Dann replied. "Take it easy."

Dann turned to two corporals assigned to his squad and tried to make out what the men were examining so closely. Both were at least a full head taller than the diminutive Dann, who stood only five feet, five inches. As Dann stepped closer he could see they were carefully studying the gear list that had been handed out moments before.

"Hey, Hambergy. They ain't got no dice on this gear list!" The brown-haired corporal spoke with a pronounced southern drawl.

"Ain't got no cards listed either," the taller, blond-haired man responded with a laugh. "We'll just have to add them ourselves."

"Howdy, boys." Dann sauntered up to the two men. "My name's Dann. Russell Dann. I guess I'm going to be your squad leader."

"Well, I guess you are," the brown-haired man replied, turning toward Dann and looking at him suspiciously. "My name's Chuck Newsome and this here's Hambergy," he said, gesturing with his thumb.

"It's Hamberger. Gary Hamberger," the blond man said affably.

"Nice to meet ya both. Sounds like you guys plan on being prepared for this mssion."

"Well, ole Hambergy here rolls a mean pair of dice, and we're afraid he might lose his touch being without 'em too long. And I'll tell ya somethin', Dann. I don't plan to play no solitaire with these cards I'm bringing along," Newsome said as he pulled a crisp deck of Players from his breast pocket and fluttered the edges with his thumb.

Dann chuckled at the antics of the two men and thought that, with these jokers around, there weren't going to be too many dull moments out at Camp Desert Rock.

"How'd you guys get on this mission?" Dann inquired.

"Well, I'll tell ya," Newsome drawled. "When I saw those orders asking for volunteers come through yesterday, I jest put my name right down on that there list."

"My C.O.," said Hamberger. "He volunteered me. How 'bout you?"

"My C.O. volunteered me too. Guess he was tired of me talkin' smart to him!" Dann chortled. "He's probably hoping I won't come back."

"Well, maybe we'll find us a couple of sweet ladies out in Vegas to take care of us and we won't come back!" Newsome interjected.

"We going to Las Vegas?" Dann asked with surprise.

"Well, this here Camp Desert Rock ain't too far at all from Vegas," Newsome answered. "And I sure do plan to check out that little ole town. Country boys like me from Virginny don't get much chance to see a real-live gamblin' town where it's open season on everything."

"Yeah," said Hamberger, "and I'm going to see how my shootin' stands up in a crap game with real pros."

Standing nearby, Lieutenant Ginn was amused as he listened to the three corporals discussing their assignment to Task Force Big Bang. He had followed a rather circuitous route himself to the provisional company.

An Army brat born at Walter Reed Army Hospital in Washington, D.C., Ginn spent his youth going from one Army base to another as his doctor father was transferred to various posts. He graduated from Leavenworth (Kansas) High School and then followed his father into the Army by accepting an appointment to West Point, graduating with the class of 1954. After that he attended Airborne and Ranger school at Fort Benning, Georgia, and was then assigned as the aide to the commander of U.S. Forces in Puerto Rico, Major General William Verbeck.

Early in 1957, Verbeck was ordered to Brazil to take over the post of Lieutenant General Robert Sink, head of the Joint U.S. Advisory Command. Sink was heading for Fort Bragg and the command of the 18th Airborne Corps. Originally, Ginn was supposed to accompany Verbeck to his new assignment, but there was a hitch. Two other military aides were already stationed in Brazil. One was a pilot and the other a Portuguese language expert. Verbeck would be needing both a pilot and a linguist in Brazil. He didn't need Ginn.

Ginn wasn't sure what was going to happen to him. U.S. troops in

Puerto Rico were quickly being phased out that year. There wasn't much call for an infantry officer without any infantry troops. About a month before Verbeck's expected transfer to Brazil, both he and Sink were ordered to a commanders' meeting at Fort Amador in the Panama Canal Zone. Ginn accompanied Verbeck to the meeting and arranged to stay with a former West Point classmate near the fort.

Neither Verbeck nor Sink cared much for the man who was their immediate superior. They rarely bothered to attend the quarterly meetings and instead used the opportunity to get together, drink and have a good time. The junior officers joked that both of the generals must have had hollow legs because they could guzzle a quart of liquor and barely whet their whistles.

When they arrived at the Canal Zone, the two generals were housed together in the senior officers' chateau, a well-appointed mansion reserved for visiting brass. Of course, as was their custom, both men quickly began trying to drink each other under the table. Ginn, recognizing that the occasion might afford the answer to his dilemma if he arranged it right, buttonholed the mess sergeant in charge of the chateau and gave him some very special orders.

"Now, listen," Ginn said, passing the sergeant a slip of paper. "When the generals are intoxicated, but before either one of them passes out, I want you to give me a call at this number."

"Yes, sir," the sergeant said with a smirk. "You can count on me."

About nine o'clock that evening, Ginn was just finishing dinner when the phone rang.

"Lieutenant Ginn?" the voice on the other end of the line asked. "This is Sergeant Reed, sir. I think the generals are just about the way you want them."

"Thank you, sergeant. I appreciate your call. Ask General Verbeck to come to the phone, would you?"

A moment later Ginn heard the receiver click as it was lifted. "This is General Verbeck," said the general thickly.

"Lieutenant Ginn here, sir," Ginn replied sprightly. "What would you think of the idea of me going to Fort Bragg as General Sink's aide? He's authorized two and only has one."

"Hang on," Verbeck answered. "I'll check."

Only a few seconds later the general was back at the phone.

"Bob thinks it's a great idea. You take care of all the details."

Early the next morning Ginn went to the offices of the Canal Zone's adjutant general and dictated orders to a clerk transferring himself to General Sink's command. What Ginn didn't know then was that his tour of duty with Sink was destined to be short-lived thanks to the same characteristics of the officer that had led to the arrangement in the first place — a penchant for liquor.

Ginn liked his new job at Fort Bragg. But apparently the young lieutenant's father, a brigadier general in the Army Medical Corps, didn't.

The senior Ginn was one-of-a-kind. By 1957 he was married to his third wife and was getting ready to retire from the service. In Korea, General Ginn commanded the Army's Mobile Army Surgical Hospitals (M*A*S*H) and earned a well-deserved reputation as a fun-loving, hard-loving, hard-drinking man.

General Ginn came to Fort Bragg to visit his son during the summer of 1957. Both were invited to General Sink's quarters for drinks, where the two generals talked over old times. While the generals blithely downed cocktail after cocktail, Ginn listened with polite interest to their oft-told tales. Finally, the elder Ginn turned to the subject that was really on his mind.

"You know, Bob. Louis here's been an aide too long," Ginn said as his son listened with a mixture of horror and astonishment. "He needs a field command with some troops under him. You ought to get rid of him."

"Think you're right, Lou," said Sink with a conspiratorial smile. "I'll take care of it."

The next day Lieutenant Ginn reported to work early, hoping against hope that the previous evening's conversation between his father and Sink had been lost in an alcoholic blackout. But Sink was his usual alert self that morning, looking none the worse for wear. As soon as Ginn walked into the general's office and cheerfully said "Good morning, sir," he knew he was sunk. Sink looked up from his desk and spoke curtly: "Louis. Your orders have already been cut. Report to HQ at the Eighty-second. I've enjoyed having you here, but I agree with your father. You need a command."

It seemed that every time a couple of generals got together for a good drunk, Ginn found himself with a new job. The lieutenant was assigned as the executive officer of C Company of the 505th only a few weeks before the provisional company was formed. Because he was new and had few duties and a lot of free time, he was a logical choice. Ginn was looking forward to the excitement of the atomic-bomb blast and the change of scenery.

Captain Stovall's voice calling his name brought Ginn back to the present. He crossed the raised platform to where the captain was standing with Crites.

"Lou," Stovall said. "I want you and Bill here to make sure our jeeps get over to Pope tomorrow morning and loaded aboard the transport."

"Be glad to, sir," Ginn replied. "Is there anything else I can do?"

"Yeah. Make sure the guys over at the motor pool put some 50-weight oil into those jeeps. It gets mighty hot on that desert."

"I'll do that, sir." Ginn and Crites headed out the door and into the hot, muggy North Carolina air.

Dann walked back to his company area at Old Division and asked the wiremen in the communications shack to finish the inventory he had started the day before. As communications chief for his unit, Dann kept the company's radios in good repair. He knew there was little that could go wrong the few days he was to be in Nevada.

Crossing over to the barracks, Dann bounded up the stairs two at a time to the second floor. In the small cubicle he shared with another corporal, he began packing up the gear needed for the mission. Carefully, Dann stowed his field gear — the heaviest items on the bottom — into his duffel bag.

He carefully cleaned and oiled his M–1 rifle, then sat down to write his parents a brief letter. Dann wasn't much of a letter writer, but he felt guilty if he didn't pen a note to his folks once in a while since his mother, Leona, was a faithful correspondent who wrote once or twice a week to keep him up-to-date on the family news.

The sixth of ten children born to Theodore and Leona Dann, Russell was raised in the small farming town of Nashua, Iowa. The town's claim to fame is that it is the locale of "The Little Brown Church in the Vale," immortalized in song by William Pitts and popularized as a Protestant hymn by the gospel-singing Weatherwax Brothers.

Always a voracious reader, Russell was a bright but disinterested student. He despised the boredom of his schoolwork and avoided it studiously, preferring instead to wander the banks of the nearby Little Cedar River with his brother Tom. Consistently playing hooky, Tom was dubbed "Tom Sawyer" by his schoolmates, and Russell, who had thick, black hair and a toothy smile, quickly earned the nickname "Huck."

Two months after he reached the age of 18, in December 1954, Dann enlisted in the Army Reserve. Three months later he quit school in his junior year and transferred to the Regular Army. From Nashua, Dann and his friend Blair Pratt traveled by bus to Camp Chaffee, Arkansas, for eight weeks of basic training. Then the pair were off to Fort Bragg for eight weeks of airborne infantry training. After that the two newly designated privates first class traveled to Fort Benning, Georgia, for jump school.

Pratt didn't make it through the rigorous training of the parachute battalion, but Dann did, graduating on September 16, 1955. By now the Iowa youth was a well-trained soldier. He was qualified as an "expert" rifleman with the standard M–1 rifle, recoilless rifle, light machine gun, heavy machine gun and the .45 caliber automatic pistol. From Fort Benning it was back to Fort Bragg, where Dann, his jump wings clipped above his left breast pocket, reported for duty as a wireman in A Company of the 505th Airborne Infantry regiment. There he stayed until Task Force Big Bang was formed, rising to the rank of corporal and earning the job of company communications chief.

Dann prided himself on the fact that he was a good soldier, regardless of what Captain Hill thought of him. Only two months earlier, in June, Hill's predecessor had recommended Dann for the battalion soldier-of-the-month award and the corporal had won the honor.

Dann was small, but solidly built. A wiry 130-pounder, he had a powerful, deep and gravelly voice that belied his size. The timbre of his voice was a boon to his military career. When he barked out orders, he could be heard clearly across a parade field and usually was picked to call cadence during his company's morning exercises. Dann had all the qualities a soldier was supposed to have. He followed orders to the letter without question. He was adept at his job, bright and, above all, he was gung-ho.

The next morning, August 12, 1957, the 163 paratroopers and seven officers rode by bus to Pope Air Force Base, where the C–124 Globemaster awaited them. At the time, Globemasters were the newest, biggest and best transports the Air Force had. A four-engine, prop-driven aircraft, the plane could carry an entire fully equipped company of paratroopers and several vehicles up to a half ton in size. The plane was divided into two decks inside. Rows of canvas slings lined the bulkheads on both sides of the plane on both decks.

During an airborne assault, the plane would make two passes over the drop zone. On the first pass the troops on the lower deck would jump out the rear door in "sticks" ("stick" is a group of men assigned to stay together or proceed in a certain manner) starting with the man who last loaded on the plane. Then, while the plane circled around for the second pass, the troopers on the top deck would climb down to the lower level and jump out the door.

At Pope, a huge cargo hatch in the plane's nose was opened and the company's quarter-ton jeeps were driven up the ramp into the Globemaster's interior. Dann helped secure the jeeps with chains to mooring slots built into the plane's aluminum deck. After watching the aircraft's crew ride an elevator to the cockpit, Dann walked toward the plane's tail, climbed the ladder to the top deck and took his seat on the port side.

When Dann felt the momentary jerk that signaled the plane's wheels had lifted off the ground, he looked around him to see that Hamberger was absent-mindedly shaking a pair of dice in his palm, waiting for the plane to reach its cruising altitude so he could get up a game of craps with his fellow soldiers. Next to him, Newsome was canvassing all the nearby troopers to see who wanted to join in the game.

The pilot's voice crackled over the loudspeaker as the plane reached its cruising altitude.

"The smoking lamp is lit. Go ahead and light up. And if any of you stump-jumpers [paratroopers] back there want to see what things are like on the flight deck, you're welcome to come forward one or two at a time."

Dann reached for the pack of Lucky Strikes in his right breast pocket and took one out. He tamped the end of the cigarette on his thumbnail, lighted a match and inhaled deeply. The cigarette helped calm his nerves, but Dann still felt naked without his parachute and kept looking around for his harness, even though he knew it wasn't there.

He stuck his hand into his hip pocket and pulled out a frayed copy of "Armed Forces Talk" that a friendly first sergeant from Baker Company had given him when he learned that Dann was heading for Camp Desert

Rock. The top sergeant had participated in Exercise Desert Rock IV two years earlier and thought the young corporal might like to know what the atomic tests were like. The magazine, published by the Pentagon on September 19, 1952, was already three years old when the sergeant got it from a friend in 1955, but it still had some useful information. Dann settled back and began to read.

"This week's *Talk* takes you directly to Camp Desert Rock for an eye-witness account of an atomic burst.

"The area around Camp Desert Rock is a genuine wasteland. It's what Gordon Dean, head of the Atomic Energy Commission, described as a 'good place to throw used razor blades.' " Dann read on, concentrating on the section of the article concerning radiation. The corporal wished he had paid closer attention to the lectures of his science teachers in high school.

"If you are like most of the observers at Desert Rock, you will be a little worried at first about the dangers of radiation. Maybe you have read books in which it is claimed that areas under an atomic blast will be uninhabitable for 20 years, 50 years, a century. This is not true. The radiation from an atomic weapon, when burst in the air, is all gone in a minute and a half. After that time, no significant radiation exists on the ground."

Dann was glad to read that. He had heard stories at Bragg that previous participants in the atomic exercises had come back sterile. But Dann dismissed the talk as idle gossip. He continued the article, reading over and over again the description of the Army's Chemical, Biological and Radiological (CBR) monitors. Dann thought to himself that the monitoring job was one that he wouldn't mind having. It was a logical progression from his job in electronics.

"The radiation for which these CBR monitors are looking will exist in the form of radioactive dust particles. Dust may be on your shoes, on your clothes or in your hair, so that when you come back, you too are radioactive. These low level radiation dust particles on your clothes and shoes may be removed by brushing off the dust with an ordinary broom. If you get rid of the dust, you get rid of the radiation."

It seemed like sound advice to Dann. Another section of the article mentioned more thorough decontamination measures, which Dann mentally filed away for future reference — just in case he was dosed with radiation.

"If you are alive and uninjured after being near an A-bomb blast you needn't worry too much about the flash radiation. The decontamination problem is relatively simple, although there is no chemical or medical method of neutralizing the radiation. Just use good old-fashioned soap and water — the hotter the water and the stronger the soap the better. If you get rid of the dirt from yourself and your equipment, you get rid of the radiation."

Sticking the magazine back in his pocket, Dann lighted up another cigarette and leaned over to watch the crap game being played on the deck at his feet. Hamberger was winning.

It was a smooth flight west that day. The sky was a clear blue, dotted only sparsely with white puffs of clouds far below. As the hours wore on, Dann's nervousness began to subside. He joined in a game of nickel-ante blackjack with Newsome and Hamberger, both of whom seemed oblivious to anything but the cards spread out before them. Dann found that if he too concentrated on the cards, his anxious thoughts about the airworthiness of the plane and what lay ahead in Nevada seemed to drift away.

After a light box lunch of sandwiches and fruit provided by the aircraft crew, Dann drained his paper coffee cup in one gulp and walked toward the plane's nose. There he boarded the small crew elevator and rode it up to the flight deck. He chatted briefly with the pilots and received assurances that the plane was performing according to specifications. The navigator pointed out the flight path of the plane on his charts and surprised Dann by telling him they would soon be making a scheduled stop at Tinker Air Force Base near Oklahoma City for refueling.

Dann hurried aft to spread the word of the stop at Tinker and buckle his seat belt. Twisting around and gazing from the porthole behind him, he could see the checkered pattern of the Oklahoma fields as the plane gradually dropped in altitude. He tried to guess what crops were growing in the various areas, judging that the amber squares in the checkboard were undoubtedly corn fields and the bright green ones either alfalfa or soybeans.

It was midafternoon when the Globemaster touched down at Tinker, jostling the paratroopers as the plane's rubber tires struck the runway. The soldiers filed out of the rear door, glad for the opportunity to stretch their legs.

Apparently there was some problem with one of the Globemaster's engines, because the troopers were stalled at Tinker for several hours. They passed the time at a cafeteria near the runway, eating, playing cards and listening to the latest tunes on the jukebox.

Finally the soldiers loaded back aboard their plane and took off on the final leg of their journey to Indian Springs Air Force Base, a small outpost paralleling a range of mountains 23 miles from Camp Desert Rock. Though the Army camp had an airfield of its own, the runway wasn't long or sturdy enough to support a landing by a plane the size of the C–124. The Desert Rock airstrip was used mostly by small commuter planes ferrying scientists back and forth between the Nevada Test Site and the government's Los Alamos Scientific Laboratory in New Mexico.

Dann was fascinated by the gradual change in terrain as the Globemaster flew due west toward Nevada. Oklahoma was lush and colorful, in the heart of the nation's farm belt. But as the plane chased the setting sun across the Texas panhandle and passed over New Mexico and into Arizona, the land far below seemed to meld into a swirling mass of brown and beige, only occasionally broken by the snaking bends of rivers that looked from the air like tiny threads.

As darkness enveloped the sky, the crap and card games wound down and many of the soldiers napped or sat quietly talking and smoking cigarettes. What only the officers of the company knew was that the paratroopers on that plane were destined to become test subjects — guinea pigs — for psychological stress tests administered by the Army's Human Resources Research Organization. And what not even the officers knew then was that within a few weeks some 80 of the assembled soldiers would have the dubious distinction of standing unprotected, closer to the blast of an atomic bomb than anyone in history — who lived to tell about it.

1

BORN IN SECRECY

The "Atomic Age" was born in secrecy. With a 1939 mandate from President Franklin D. Roosevelt to beat Germany in the race to harness the destructive power of splitting atoms, U.S. scientists were brought together with a few brilliant Europeans who had fled Nazism. They began work under the aegis of the Manhattan District of the U.S. Army Corps of Engineers.

Hidden from public view by elaborate fronts and cover stories, the members of the so-called Manhattan Project huddled in laboratories scattered across the nation, struggling to unlock the secrets of fission. The project made it necessary for an entire new industry to be created covertly.

In only a matter of months, factories, laboratories and manufacturing plants sprung up in such varied locations as New York City; Hanford, Washington; Oak Ridge, Tennessee; St. Louis; Los Alamos, New Mexico; Washington, D.C.; and Chicago. Thousands of construction workers, assembly line laborers, physicists, metallurgists, chemists, engineers, administrators, managers, typists and clerks were needed for the effort.

Finally, at the closely guarded Los Alamos laboratory of physicist Dr. J. Robert Oppenheimer, a prototype bomb was assembled during the early summer months of 1945. In the years preceding, all the work and thought invested in the bomb had been only an intellectual exercise. Germany had already surrendered, and though the war appeared to be winding down that summer, the scientists felt compelled to prove their theories right or wrong.

At 5:30 A.M. on July 16, 1945, the theories were put to the test. While nervous scientists and skeptical military observers lay flat on the ground with their eyes protected by gray-lensed goggles, a 19-kiloton atomic bomb was electronically detonated 20 miles away on a 100-foot tower above the white sands of the desert near Alamogordo, New Mexico. The searing flash of the explosion was seen 180 miles away.

Questions about the bright, predawn light were fielded by government experts who explained the phenomenon away as the explosion of an ammunition dump. The existence of the atom bomb remained a tightly held secret — that is, until nearly three weeks later on August 5, 1945, when an Army Air Corps B-29 bomber called the *Enola Gay* dropped a 13-kiloton uranium-fueled bomb on the Japanese city of Hiroshima. Four days later a 23-kiloton plutonium-fueled bomb devastated the Japanese industrial center of Nagasaki and the war quickly ended with Japan's unconditional surrender.

Oppenheimer later recalled at a congressional hearing that "many times we scientists thought the war might end before we had a bomb. But some of us did not stop, because we wanted the world to see the atomic bomb. It was, to us, the greatest argument for world peace."

It was an immensely forceful argument, but it did little to promote international harmony. Instead, the Japanese bombings only goaded the Russians into stepping up their own development of atomic weapons and renewed the resolve of strategic planners in the United States to keep details of the Los Alamos successes in the hands of Americans. Though Secretary of War Henry L. Stimson, a Republican who served in the cabinets of Taft and Hoover, argued in 1945 that the United States should share its precious secret with our wartime Russian allies, he was overruled by President Harry Truman, who had a healthy distrust of the Kremlin leaders.

Only 40 days after the atomic bomb destroyed Nagasaki, a specially equipped amphibious tank, its treads squeaking and clanking, rumbled ashore at Sasebo Harbor on the Japanese island of Kyushu. Aboard were 13 hand-picked, battle-hardened U.S. Marines. All were military police and crack machine gunners. They were the first Americans to set foot on the Japanese island since the war began. Their job was to travel all over the island, collecting the signatures of local officials on surrender papers. The mayors were required to attest, in writing, that the Marines would not be fired on when they landed.

Corporal Harry Coppola, a 25-year-old native of Revere, Massachusetts, was among the Marines who landed on Kyushu. Coppola was a veteran of the Marine landings on Guam and Iwo Jima, two of the South

Pacific's fiercest battles. On Iwo Jima, his steady machine gunner's hand had provided cover fire while Marines from the Fifth Division raised the American flag on Mount Suribachi. At Third Division headquarters on Guadalcanal, Coppola had attended a crash course in rudimentary Japanese. He had proven himself cool under fire and could converse in the enemy's language. That made him a natural for the Kyushu mission.

After only two days, the Marines had traveled the length and breadth of the island and collected the necessary signatures. The officer in charge radioed the main body of Marines lying out of range of Japanese coastal batteries 11 miles offshore that it was safe to land. The Second Marine "Pioneer" Engineer Battalion thundered ashore later that day, augmented by a detachment of U.S. Navy Seabees. The mission of the engineers, equipped with bulldozers and other heavy machinery, was to help clean up the terrible destruction wrought by the atomic bombs.

Corporal Coppola and another Japanese-language specialist were dispatched to Omura Air Base, 11 miles from the bombed-out city of Nagasaki. At night, they slept in a demolished barracks that once housed Japanese pilots. Across the road, at another barracks, U.S. Marine pilots slept between missions ferrying food and medical supplies to the island. It was there that Coppola met Tyrone Power, Hollywood heart throb and a Marine flier, who amazed his fellow leathernecks by ignoring base restrictions with impunity. Power ventured off base almost daily, armed only with a pistol, in search of sake and women. Apparently the actor was determined to maintain his well-deserved reputation as a Lothario.

By day, Coppola patroled what was left of the city of Nagasaki. All that remained of a once massive industrial center were piles of rubble, ashes, dust and dead bodies. The official casualty reports listed 74,000 killed in the city. Everywhere Coppola looked there were bodies. Arms and legs jutted out from beneath the piles of ash. In nearly every open space, the grisly, bloated and burned bodies littered the landscape, festering in the hot sun. The fetid smell of seared rotting flesh assaulted the senses.

Thousands of Japanese citizens tried to stream into the dead city in search of relatives and friends. But the Marines turned them away. It would have been impossible for them to locate anyone anyhow. There were no street signs. There were no streets. All that remained were charred heaps of concrete, steel and wood.

Fourteen days after landing on the island, both Coppola and the other

Marine assigned to patrol duty became violently ill. Dizzy and nauseous, their bellies burned with bile. Neither man could keep any food down. They became weak and unsteady. Both complained to their commanding officer that they couldn't carry out their duties.

At first, Coppola attributed his sickness to the stench of dead bodies. The smell overpowered him during the first few days in the city. He often retched his meals up, only minutes after eating. But in time Coppola was able to steel himself against the awful stink. When the nausea continued, he knew something else was wrong. Perhaps it was the dust he inhaled or contaminated drinking water.

Whatever it was that had him doubled over with stomach pains, Coppola desperately wanted it to end. If he had been cautioned about the effects of radiation exposure, perhaps Coppola would have known that the nausea and dizziness were distinct signs of radiation sickness. But the Marines had received no training in atomic effects.

On November 9, 1945, the two men shipped out for San Diego. On the trip home, their nausea subsided. The Nagasaki veterans seemingly received special handling by the brass. A jeep awaited them on the San Diego pier and they were chauffeured to Oceanside Marine Corps Base. After a cursory physical, both men were summarily discharged from the Marine Corps only two days after arriving in California. Others lounged around the base for weeks and months, waiting to be processed back into civilian life.

In the year after the Japanese bombings, U.S. atomic scientists detonated two more bombs on the remote Pacific isle of Bikini. The members of the Manhattan Project, some remorseful about their participation in the destruction wrought by their invention, drifted away from the government to positions in academia and industry. Truman recognized the need for keeping the country's long strides into the new Atomic Age firmly under government control. In early October 1946 he established an Atomic Energy Committee to advise him and oversee the nation's atomic weapons development program.

With five prominent Americans chosen to make up the organization, the committee was given broad powers and a scepter to wield over other agencies of the government — a secrecy stamp. An almost paranoiac suspicion about Russia's intentions had supplanted the wartime fear that the Germans would develop atom bombs before anyone else. The Atomic Energy Committee, later elevated to the status of presidential commission, at first was allowed to deliberate in total secrecy, unimpeded by the normal peacetime procedure of congressional oversight.

Tapped for the chairmanship of the new commission was David Lilienthal. A gregarious, thoughtful and creative administrator, Lilienthal had distinguished himself years earlier when he was chosen by Roosevelt to shepherd the Tennessee Valley Authority during the halcyon days of the New Deal. A graduate of DePauw University and later a member of the Wisconsin Public Service Commission, Lilienthal championed the concept of the "cheap kilowatt" at TVA and was a likely and logical choice to head the commission.

In April and May of 1948, government scientists tested three more atomic bombs in the South Pacific on the coral-reefed Eniwetok atoll, once a vital communications station during the war against Japan. The tests were code-named Sandstone and though bombs two and three times the size of the Hiroshima weapon were successfully detonated, the Army general in charge of the operation complained about the logistical problems imposed by the long supply lines to the site. Project Nutmeg, a study of possible U.S. sites for the testing program was immediately begun by the Armed Forces Special Weapons Project, an organization made up of atomic-bomb specialists from all of the military services.

After a year the study was inconclusive, but the military planners did make a preliminary judgment: from all of the information available, the arid southwestern part of the continental United States seemed to be the preferred location. The AEC put off a decision on the plan and laid aside the Nutmeg study in 1949 for later consideration "in the event of an emergency." An emergency — war in Korea — wasn't long in coming. But even before events in Asia placed a new urgency on the selection of a continental atomic test site, the Russians exploded their own atomic bomb in August 1949 and another issue deeply split the ranks of the AEC.

The dilemma facing the commission was whether to advise President Truman to give the go-ahead for the development of another terrible new weapon — the hydrogen bomb. The commission was sharply divided. On one side, Lilienthal argued that the U.S. should exhaust every means of reaching an agreement with Russia to outlaw atomic warfare before producing hydrogen bombs. Lilienthal recommended a reasoned approach. He suggested appealing over the heads of the Kremlin leaders to the Russian people. They, Lilienthal insisted, would force Premier Joseph Stalin to come to terms.

But Lilienthal was opposed by his old adversary on the commission —
Rear Admiral Lewis Strauss. From the beginning of the organization,
Strauss and Lilienthal had consistently been on opposite sides of almost
every argument. A one-time secretary to President Herbert Hoover,
wartime aide to Navy Secretary James Forrestal and a prominent member
of the New York banking firm of Kuhn, Loeb and Company, the vain and
strident Strauss regularly clashed behind closed doors with the more
cautious Lilienthal.

At first, Strauss was the lone Republican dissenter on the pre-
dominantly Democratic commission. But by 1950 there were more
Republicans on the commission than Democrats and the pro–hydrogen
bomb position was supported by both Truman's National Security
Council and the newly created Joint Committee on Atomic Energy of
Congress.

Strauss argued forcefully that the Soviets couldn't be trusted. After all,
they had refused to abide by proposals calling for a mutual inspection of
atomic stockpiles by U.S. and Russian experts. Strauss convincingly
insisted that "we cannot afford not to make the new hydrogen bomb. We
must maintain our superiority over any possible aggressor. That is the
chief hope left for peace."

The majority of commission members bought Strauss's argument,
and, apparently, so did President Truman, who gave the go-ahead for the
H-bomb's development only a week later. The next month, Lilienthal
resigned from the commission; Strauss soon followed to become a
consultant to the Joint Committee, and Truman began looking for a likely
successor.

To head the commission Truman chose Gordon Dean, a preacher's son
from Seattle, and an aggressive young Justice Department lawyer who,
while relatively new to the commission, sided with Strauss against
Lilienthal during the H-bomb debate.

In the next few months, tensions between East and West flared, North
Korea invaded South Korea in late June and U.S. military planners began
considering the use of tactical atomic weapons to end the conflict. But the
South Pacific islands were far from the weapons fabrication plant in Los
Alamos and unprotected from the prying eyes of Russians. So Project
Nutmeg was resurrected.

In early August 1950, 24 of the nation's top physicists, meteorologists
and health experts met at the Los Alamos Scientific Laboratory (LASL)

for a daylong discussion of the possible radiological hazards posed to the public by locating an atomic test site within the shores of the continental United States.

Among others, the meeting was attended by such luminaries as Dr. Enrico Fermi, one of the leaders of the Manhattan Project and a world-renowned physicist; Dr. Alvin C. Graves, physicist and director of the AEC's bomb testing program; Dr. William E. Ogle, physicist and director of LASL; and Dr. Edward Teller, another Manhattan Project veteran, then hard at work as the architect of a hydrogen-bomb development program.

Dr. Graves opened the meeting by setting up a few ground rules. First, he said, the discussion would be limited to the radiation hazards associated with using the Tonopah Bombing and Gunnery Range near Las Vegas, Nevada, for the test site. Graves pointedly added that "these considerations are from a radiological point of view only" and cautioned the gathered scientists to omit "psychological and political" implications from their arguments.

The health risks involved were summarized by Major General James P. Cooney, an Army medical doctor who specialized in radiology. Cooney suggested that "a rapidly administered integrated dose of 25 roentgens* (25r) wholebody radiation can be taken as an emergency acceptable dose if received only once." The general went on to say that he thought Dr. Shields Warren, head of the AEC's Division of Biology and Medicine, would go along with that dosage limit and argued that it was "generally accepted by the medical profession that this amount of radiation will cause no disability, regardless of the physical condition of the recipient."

Dr. Cooney gave the assembled experts a quick course in the biological effects of radiation. He patiently explained that a person could receive up to 100r of radiation and still be "reasonably certain that no permanent injury will result." From an ordinary X-ray, said the general, "a person receives less than one roentgen; a gastrointestinal examination may involve as much as 45 to 50r."

At that point Cooney was interrupted by Dr. Thomas White, head of

---

*A roentgen is an international unit of "gamma" or "X-ray" radiation named for the German physicist Wilhelm Konrad Roentgen (1845–1923).

LASL's health division, who raised questions about the danger of ingesting radioactive materials through the mouth or the nose at doses of 25r. Cooney dismissed the doctor's worries by saying that at the Eniwetok tests during Operation Sandstone three years earlier, it appeared that "one would have to ingest a kilogram of the material immediately under the shot in order to ingest enough plutonium to cause physical damage."

The meteorologists at the meeting assured everyone that it was "almost impossible for the atomic cloud to cause a rainstorm" and that previous tests at Bikini made it appear unlikely that "the fallout of radioactive particles would seed natural clouds in the vicinity" and rain radiation down on areas beneath the atomic clouds. The weather experts cautioned, however, that tests should be avoided during the rainy and snowy winter months.

A satisfactory day for a blast, they explained, would be a "day in which the wind at all levels blows from either the southwest or the southeast . . . that way it would miss Las Vegas." The meteorologists noted that the only places to worry about in terms of radiation were those "within a radius of 150 miles" since they were certain that fallout outside that radius would be negligible.

Days when there was a variable wind, rain downwind or weather currents that would bring the lower portion of an atomic cloud over a nearby town were to be avoided. But even those criteria weren't exactly rigid. One of the weather experts explained that a part of the cloud could pass over Las Vegas without any danger if it was small enough to insure that "25r could not be carried down even in the case of a total rainout."

During the afternoon session of the meeting, Dr. Enrico Fermi broached the subject which earlier in the day had been declared taboo by Graves. "I'm sorry to bring up psychological implications," Fermi said, "but it's my impression that if conditions are such that 10 roentgens will be received by people under the atomic cloud, they should be warned to stay indoors, take showers and so forth."

Disregarding Fermi's worries, the group concluded in its final report that the famed Italian scientist was concerned about a risk based "on somewhat pessimistic estimates. This risk," the report stated, "is not a probability that anyone will be killed or even hurt, but it does contain the probability that people will receive perhaps a little more radiation than medical authorities say is absolutely safe — six roentgens."

At the time, the so-called threshold theory of radiation effects was in vogue and generally accepted throughout the medical and scientific community. This theory held that human beings could receive radiation up to a certain threshold point without suffering any discernible ill effects. The safety threshold of 6r was arrived at on the basis of animal and human studies that showed, at most, only "temporary" blood changes when that amount of radiation was received.

In deference to Fermi, the final report of the Los Alamos meeting included a sort of gratuitous alibi clause: "Fermi felt that our conclusions should stress the extreme uncertainty of the elements we had to go on, and that we did our best with these, that the group is attempting to agree on physical facts."

In the end, the assembled scientists sanguinely concluded that "a tower burst bomb having a yield of 25kt could be detonated without exceeding the allowed emergency tolerance dose of six to 12r outside a 180 degree test area sector 100 miles in radius."

Incorporating the results of the Los Alamos meeting into a memorandum, the President's National Security Council directed the AEC and the Defense Department to recommend a site for atomic weapons tests in November 1950. The NSC's Special Committee on Atomic Energy Matters recognized that test sites outside the U.S. could offer certain advantages because of their remoteness. Larger bombs could be detonated without worrying about fallout over populated areas. But sites like Eniwetok atoll in the South Pacific and Amchitka in the Aleutian Islands off the coast of Alaska were only acceptable if the testing program could be carried out at a leisurely pace with plenty of time to ferry men and materials to the remote locations.

Time was a luxury the atom-bomb testing program did not have in 1950. U.S. troops had landed in Korea in July and forced the invading North Koreans back above the 38th parallel dividing the two countries. But the battles were costly, and by November 1950 General Douglas MacArthur, commander of U.S. Forces in Korea, reported that Chinese Communist troops were fighting as proxies of the North Koreans. At AEC headquarters in Washington, urgency was a prime factor in deciding where and when to resume the bomb testing program.

Early in December 1950 the AEC's Division of Military Application prepared a detailed report on possible sites for the testing program and spelled out the commission's options. They decided an ideal test site would be an area of remote flat land, near Los Alamos, under government control and with enough water and electricity to support needed base camps and scientific instruments.

The AEC's military advisers reported to the commission that atomic shots of a size equivalent to 25,000 tons of TNT (25kt) "can certainly, and shots up to 50,000 tons can probably, be detonated within acceptable safety limits in the continental U.S." The advisers determined that by carefully studying blasts in the 25kt to 50kt range, estimates could be made for yields of even bigger blasts "and the above limits may eventually be raised considerably."

There were five locations that met most of the criteria: the Alamogordo–White Sands Guided Missile Range in New Mexico, where the first atom bomb was detonated; the Dugway Proving Ground in Utah; the Las Vegas–Tonopah Bombing and Gunnery Range; another area in Nevada about 50 miles wide and extending from the city of Fallon to Eureka; and the Pamlico Sound–Camp Lejeune area in North Carolina.

For a variety of reasons, all of the sites except Las Vegas were ruled out. For instance, the Alamogordo area was considered too close to Salt Lake City for safety and the North Carolina area wasn't completely under government control and was far from Los Alamos. In the end, the Division of Military Application recommended that the Tonopah Bombing and Gunnery Range near Las Vegas was the best option since it was the largest area of all the sites, was under complete control of the government and had the lowest population density.

Almost in passing, the military advisers made one other recommendation that over the years became a primary factor influencing nearly every decision the commission ever made about atmospheric bomb testing. "It is recognized that the problem of radiological safety is most critical in site selection," the memo to the AEC noted. "Not only must high safety factors be established in fact, *but the acceptance of these factors by the general public must be insured by judicious handling of the public information program.*" (Emphasis added.)

On December 13, 1950, AEC Chairman Gordon Dean sent the National Security Council a review of the report by the Division of Military Application and advised the council that the AEC's budget then under consideration by Congress contained a million-dollar request "for the initiation of development of a continental test site." Dean proposed choosing the Tonopah Bombing and Gunnery Range as the atomic weapons test site and suggested that the text of his memo was "suitable for presenting this recommendation to the President." Five days later Truman approved Dean's proposal.

But while Dean's relations with the White House seemed almost blessed with an absence of friction, things weren't going quite so smoothly during budget hearings on Capitol Hill. At a secret session of the House Appropriations Committee, Dean aggressively defended the high cost of weapons development by arguing that "every nickel of the three billion dollars we have spent on atom and H-bomb development in the last four years is paying defense dividends." Texas Congressman Albert Thomas wasn't immediately convinced.

"What John Q. Public has in the back of his mind," Thomas asked, "is what has happened to that three billion-plus you have had in the last four years — all peacetime years?"

"I am one of John Q. Public," Dean countered, "and I wondered about the program before I came to the commission. I wondered 'How strong are we?' And I can say, as one who has come into the program, that we are in a strong position — well ahead of Russia."

Dean answered every legislator's probing question with that veiled threat — give the commission the money required or face the consequences of a rapidly expanding Russian atomic weapons program. Capitol Hill at the time was rocking under charges by Congressmen J. Parnell Thomas and Richard M. Nixon of the House Un-American Activities Committee that Communist spies and Russian agents were infesting the government and defense industries, that, indeed, the A bomb secret had been given to the Soviets.

President Truman established the employee loyalty program, determined to insure that "no disloyal person should be employed by our government." Federal Bureau of Investigation Director J. Edgar Hoover bluntly warned that Communists loyal to Moscow were trying to overthrow the U.S. government. Winston Churchill declared that "from Stettin in the Baltic to Trieste in the Adriatic, an Iron Curtain has descended across the Continent." In a sort of unspoken game of political blackmail, the legislators of the House Appropriations Committee were perfectly willing to give Dean what he asked for rather than risk allegations that they were "soft on the Russians."

Almost immediately after President Truman approved the AEC's test site plan in December, construction at the bombing range began in earnest. A small Air Force base of temporary buildings called Camp Mercury already existed at the southeasternmost tip of the 5,400-square-mile bombing range. The AEC quickly began negotiating with the Air Force so Mercury could be converted for atomic test purposes in time for a series of blasts planned for late the next month. The AEC also began making arrangements to relocate some civilians living on or near the test site and herds of sheep that grazed on some of the bombing range's high mesas.

By January 10, 1951, President Truman approved a series of five atomic-bomb tests, code-named Operation Ranger. While a press release was prepared at AEC headquarters, Gordon Dean, accompanied by his military adviser, broke the news to Nevada's senior senator, Patrick McCarran.

A Democrat and an immensely powerful member of the Senate Appropriations Committee, McCarran was a bombastic speaker, given to tirades against his enemies. A heavyset man with piercing eyes and a wild shock of white hair, the senator was not one to inspire ambivalent feelings in those he met. His enemies feared his wrath; his friends loved his generosity and loyalty.

AEC Chairman Dean knew better than to let McCarran find out in news accounts about the atomic bombs that were about to be set off in his home state. The chairman wisely judged that a personal "courtesy" visit from him would make future activities of the AEC in Nevada run a lot more smoothly.

Operation Ranger was a series consisting of five bombs dropped from the air during the last few days of January and the first days of February 1951. The devices ranged from 1 kiloton to 22 kilotons in size.

As anticipated in the AEC's earlier recommendations, a heavy emphasis was placed on the public relations problems engendered by the blasts. According to a report on Operation Ranger prepared by Los Alamos scientists, the "somewhat delicate public relations aspects of the affair" were carefully considered in setting levels of radiation to which the general public could be exposed. The scientists decided that 25r doses were permissible since that exposure was "no greater exposure than many people received in an only moderately complete X-ray exam."

If there was a danger of public exposures in the 25r to 50r range, the AEC scientists suggested that thought be given "to requesting people to stay in their houses, change clothes, take baths, etc. For areas where exposure above 50r may occur, consideration must of necessity be given to evacuating personnel.'' But the scientists recommended that such a drastic step shouldn't be taken "unless it is firmly regarded as essential."

The territory surrounding the test site was sparsely populated. Closest to the blast area were residents of Indian Springs and Cactus Springs, Nevada, about 25 miles southeast. Farther in that direction no one was closer than the fringes of Las Vegas, approximately 65 miles away. To the east several families were scattered along Highway 93, but none was closer than 60 miles. To the north a small community of 16 people lived at Groom Mine, 38 miles from the original shot area, on a wide expanse of sandy desert known as Frenchman's Flat.

Ten two-man radiation-monitoring teams were dispatched to the small communities that weather forecasts indicated might be under the passing atomic cloud. One team unexpectedly encountered a herd of about 50 bighorn, or mountain, sheep grazing a range of peaks about 40 miles east-southeast of the test site. Another group of monitors based in the town of Caliente, Nevada, formed a basketball team and played, not too successfully, in a local tournament. For the most part, the work of the monitors was, according to the scientific reports, "disappointing to those craving excitement, but reassuring to those wondering about the possibility of creating unsafe condition."

The first detonation of the Ranger series occurred on the morning of Saturday, January 27, 1951. Almost perfect weather conditions prevailed and the wind carried the 1 kiloton bomb's mushroom cloud eastward. Monitoring teams were able to approach ground zero within an hour and a half and found radiation levels measuring only 750 millirems (.75r or 750mr). As for the mobile teams east and northeast of the shot, "their only reward was obtaining a few readings showing levels of two or three times" the normal background radiation in the area.

The monitoring teams had trouble communicating with head-quarters either by telephone or by radio. Their equipment was inadequate, and there weren't enough phone lines at Camp Mercury to accommodate all the incoming calls. At the control point itself, the Operation Ranger report candidly admitted that "complete confusion was the order of the day."

The second shot, an 8kt device, was detonated the next morning. Because of its higher yield, this bomb "produced radiation intensities at ground zero greater than 16r per hour." The monitors in areas adjacent to the test site reported that "if a man happened to be actually in the path of the low-lying dust cloud he could measure significant amounts of activities while airborne particles, very small in size, were actually around him. When this dust cloud had passed, there seemed to be little or nothing deposited on the ground and no residual activity of any significance."

By the day after the second shot, the scientists were beginning to wear down. Many of the workers had toiled for 48 hours or longer without sleep while working steadily under extreme tension. "It was perfectly obvious," the scientists later reported, "that all personnel — scientific, monitoring and supervisory — had about reached the limit of endurance . . . there were no accidents of any consequence. It is to be devoutly hoped that it will never again be necessary to tempt fate in the same way."

The third shot, a small 1-kiloton device, was uneventful. But when another 8-kiloton bomb was set off on February 2, two storefront windows in Las Vegas 65 miles away were shattered by the blast. Levels of radiation measuring 8 millirems per hour (mr/hr) were recorded high in the Spring Mountains north of the range, but according to the AEC's criteria there wasn't any danger from those low levels. A public announcement was made in Las Vegas warning residents to stay away from windows at the time of any subsequent detonations.

Shot number five was a 22kt bomb, almost equal to the device that flattened Nagasaki. It produced radiation readings as high as 14 mr/hr immediately after the explosion when the lower portion of the cloud "practically invested Charleston Peak," the highest mountain in the area and a refuge for Las Vegans escaping the desert heat.

Though members of the general public could be exposed to as much as 25r of radiation under the AEC's policy, AEC workers were limited to a dose of only 3r. Many of the workers at Operation Ranger were needed at the next series of tests planned for the South Pacific later that year. They were limited to a total dose of 2r. The highest individual AEC worker's cumulative dosimeter recording for the test series was 3.1r.

No "significant levels" of radioactive contamination were found anywhere in the area adjacent to the test site. The monitors judged that "at none of the five shots was there evidence of fallout which might be dangerous to humans or animals within a radius covered by the mobile monitoring teams." However, several days after the blasts, measurable radioactivity did appear in the snow in New England.

The scientists weren't even slightly alarmed by the appearance of fallout in New England. Instead, they cavalierly dismissed the phenomenon by saying that the contamination simply "bears out the contention that by far the greatest part of activity is in the upper part of the cloud," and hence carried away from the test site by strong winds in the upper atmosphere. These winds almost always blow from west to east because of the constant spinning of the earth. Over the years, radioactive fallout from Nevada constantly blanketed a wide swath of the United States stretching from southwest Utah toward the northeast and New England.

The Los Alamos scientists who authored the final Ranger report made several recommendations. Among them were requests for hot showers and the strong suggestion "that at no time in the future should test operations involve nuclear detonations on successive days." They also asked for a "larger pool of experienced monitors."

The scientists didn't feel that the monitors available were really qualified. They noted that "familiarity with the various monitoring instruments does not constitute sufficient experience for men to go into areas where high and possibly dangerous levels of radiation exist." Their concern about qualified radiation monitors was admirable in 1950, but, later in the testing program, the early worries about inexperienced monitors were almost totally forgotten as poorly trained soldiers were given the opportunity to take over what was a crucial and complicated task.

The authors of the Ranger report did make one interesting admission of ignorance. The fact that one of the bombs shattered windows in Las Vegas prompted the candid assessment that "the factors controlling this are poorly understood." Of course, the admission was not a public acknowledgment, since it was deeply buried in the Ranger report — stamped SECRET.

In the midst of Operation Ranger, another bomb of a different nature exploded in bold headlines across the Atlantic. While scientists in Nevada were breaking windows with the fourth blast of the series on February 2, British physicist Klaus Fuchs was arrested in England. Fuchs admitted meeting an American agent of the Russians in New York, Boston and Sante Fe, New Mexico, during the war and passing on atom-bomb information. The guilty plea by Fuchs immediately touched off a massive hunt for the missing traitor in the U.S., culminating in the arrests of several "atom spies" by the FBI, two of whom — Julius and Ethel Rosenberg — were put to death after four years of legal wrangling.

The next month another event occurred that set the AEC on a course of action that continued as long as the commission existed — the suppression of dissenting scientific views. Arnold B. Grobman was about to publish a book titled *Our Atomic Heritage,* criticizing the AEC for failing to insist that adequate measures be taken at AEC labs to protect workers from radiation. Grobman contended that serious genetic abnormalities might result in the offspring of the nuclear workers because of their exposure to radiation. He also argued that the AEC had been remiss in encouraging publication of research results in the field because the commission's own inadequacies might be revealed.

At a closed-door meeting of the AEC on March 26, Dr. Max R. Zelle reviewed the latest knowledge available about the effects of radiation on genetics and termed the Grobman charges "possibly misleading." The commission members argued that the charges by Grobman were untrue. They verbally patted each other on the back while one by one the commissioners enumerated the financial support they had lent to genetics research.

By the end of the meeting, the commission decided to try to head off Grobman in the press, just in case his "empty" charges got any attention. In a classic case of overreaction, the members decided to prepare a statement on the "true" genetic effects of radiation to be ready for "on project" use and, if necessary, public release.

The statement, the commissioners decided, would serve to reassure any AEC workers who were worried by Grobman's allegations. In retrospect, the "Grobman affair" was an inauspicious beginning of a concerted effort that later grew by leaps and bounds to counter scientific dissent and criticism of the AEC. In later years, scientists who expressed opinions that did not conform to the AEC's party line were met with financial roadblocks, an AEC-sponsored "truth squad" and, in some cases, attempts at character assassination.

Though fears about the vulnerability of South Pacific tests led to the selection of the Nevada Test Site, the AEC didn't abandon the Pacific isles. By April 1951 a four-shot series of tests code-named Operation Greenhouse was underway at Eniwetok and Los Alamos scientists were already planning for another series of blasts to be detonated at the Nevada Test Site the following October. At an AEC meeting on Tuesday, April 17, Carroll Tyler, manager of the AEC's Santa Fe Operations Office, and Los Alamos Director Dr. Norris Bradbury presented their plan for an expansion of the facilities at Camp Mercury.

The two men explained that if the upcoming tests in Nevada were to be successful, construction on the necessary facilities had to get underway. The site desperately needed utility and operational structures, including a communications system that would prevent the sort of problems that cropped up during Operation Ranger, a control area, the erection of detonating towers and a "modest camp." To keep the dust down when the bombs exploded, they also recommended paving two of the blast areas. The total cost of the proposed construction, Tyler estimated, would exceed eight million dollars.

Dean answered the requests by diplomatically praising the efficiency and speed with which Operation Ranger was conducted on "an urgent basis" with no time to build support facilities. But Dean also explained that there seemed to be some limitations on the site itself. High-yield weapons couldn't be tested, and there were uncertainties about possible radiological hazards that might limit the site's future use. The chairman asked for detailed recommendations and warned the two men to keep expenditures to a minimum.

Eight days later the commission was presented a specific report of proposals for construction at the Nevada Test Site. An international uproar was touched off by the bomb blast at Eniwetok the week before — Asians especially were angry over the use of Pacific Ocean islands for testing — and the commissioners realized that "the international situation was such as to possibly prevent or curtail future use of Eniwetok."

This time Tyler and Bradbury's recommendations were met with a warmer response. The commissioners recommended that the target areas for ground zero of the various blasts be moved 20 miles north from Frenchman's Flat, beyond Yucca Pass to Yucca Flat, a huge expanse of desert surrounded on all sides by mountains.

The scientists on the AEC staff had concluded that the relocation would provide a greater safety factor when they were attempting to contain the uncertain radiological and fallout hazards of tower shots.

Finally, the commissioners approved the extensive development of the test site in Nevada as "necessary to the national defense and security" of the country.

The commission's concerns about safety apparently weren't too deep. In June, Dr. Shields Warren, head of the AEC's Division of Biology and Medicine, approached the commission with a plan to establish an advisory group at Los Alamos to oversee radiation problems and safety issues. In response, the commissioners closely questioned Warren about the need for such a committee. Was it possible, they wanted to know, that his own division wasn't up to snuff?

"It was concluded," read the secret minutes of the AEC meeting on June 27, 1951, "that the committee should be established initially only on a temporary basis, while its scope would be limited to such functions as the recommendation of safety criteria." The action temporarily appeased Warren, but only indicated the differences that were to divide the careful health expert from his superiors in the coming months.

The next month, Army Colonel H. McK. Roper, executive secretary of the AEC's Military Liaison Committee, sent Dean a startling request: "The three services have expressed a need for the attendance of military personnel at one of the tests of atomic weapons at the Nevada test site in the fall of 1951." The colonel explained that either an airdrop or a tower shot would effectively meet the needs of the service chiefs. The military planners wanted the opportunity to indoctrinate troops in methods of protecting themselves during atomic warfare and to observe the "psychological effects of an atomic explosion" on the soldiers. "The psychological implications of atomic weapons used close to our own front lines," Roper argued, "are unknown."

The plan was for an Army regimental combat team of 5,000 soldiers to establish an actual troop combat position close to ground zero. Then, just prior to the detonation, the troops would withdraw to a safe distance, leaving their film badges in slit trenches. As soon as it was safe, the combat team would "engage in a coordinated ground force advance over the area neutralized by the explosion."

Within two weeks, Dean replied to Roper with a letter that brought smiles to the dour faces of generals and admirals throughout the Pentagon. "Your proposal for the inclusion of a 5,000-man regimental combat team maneuver," wrote Dean, "has our complete concurrence." The chairman went on to warn Roper, however, that the military services would have to be prepared to deal with tough logistical problems. Roads were inadequate, water and communications systems were limited, and most of the available facilities were already being heavily used by the AEC.

Dean also cautioned that "the radiological safety and security implications" of the military's participation in the tests were also a factor. While willing to help, Dean pointed out that the commission was "not able to assume the burden of furnishing facilities for their [the troops'] administrative movement, security control or support."

That was enough for the Pentagon chiefs. On September 12, a convoy of trucks from the Army's Third Corps Artillery arrived at a juncture in the road a stone's throw south of Camp Mercury and established Camp Desert Rock.

A week later in Santa Fe, Carroll Tyler was designated as the "responsible officer of the AEC for the conduct of the Buster-Jangle Operation." Tyler was advised that the commission had approved the attendance of a military combat unit at the tests and was instructed to "set the criteria of time, place, radiological safety and security necessary to prevent significant interference." Tyler was also told that the commissioners wanted him to insure "strict adherence to its policy of excluding press representatives from this series of atomic tests."

The stage was set for the preliminary acts of a real-life play, which was to climax six years later when Russell Jack Dann and the other guinea pigs of the 82nd Airborne arrived at Camp Desert Rock.

2

THE HUMAN FACTOR

The specter of atomic warfare on the horizon gave rise to intriguing questions and new theories of how the threat of mutual destruction would affect the teetering balance of terror between the United States and Russia in the shaky cold war years after World War II. But even more immediate questions in the atomic warfare equation remained unanswered in the minds of strategic planners at the Pentagon — questions about the human behavior factor.

How would our own troops react to the use of tactical nuclear weapons on the battlefield? How much did our own soldiers understand about the effects of atomic bombs? Could the fears and suspicions of America's front-line troops be allayed by traditional tried-and-true indoctrination methods? These were questions strategists in the Defense Department were determined to have answered.

Late in June 1951 the Army embarked on a plan to form a Human Resources Research Office (HumRRO) that would be charged with the job of conducting research into training methods, motivation and morale, and psychological warfare techniques. George Washington University in the nation's capital won the contract to organize the office under its academic umbrella, financed entirely by the Defense Department.

The university conducted a quick but thorough search for a qualified administrator and scientist to head the operation. In July, Dr. Meredith Crawford, respected dean of the College of Arts and Sciences at Vanderbilt University, was lured from Nashville and named HumRRO director.

Crawford, who earned his psychology doctorate from Columbia University in 1935 when the field was still in its infancy, immediately began assembling a first-rate staff of experts from across the nation. The professor had to work fast; HumRRO's first assignment was to conduct a study of the attitudes and knowledge about atomic effects of soldiers involved in Exercise Desert Rock I — scheduled for October.

The HumRRO scientists planned to collect their data by distributing questionnaires to the troops before and after the maneuver. Another group of soldiers, who weren't scheduled to go to Camp Desert Rock, were also given questionnaires. Their responses were used as a "control" so the effectiveness of indoctrination lectures on the two groups could be compared.

One questionnaire, designed to find out how much information and misinformation the men had about atomic effects, was administered to 11th Airborne paratroopers at Fort Campbell, Kentucky, before they left for Camp Desert Rock. Another "quiz" was given to them following special indoctrination lectures, another after the soldiers returned from the maneuver on Yucca Flat and one more to measure their "delayed reactions" to the exercise three weeks after the troopers returned to Fort Campbell.

The HumRRO scientists weren't the only researchers interested in what psychological effect the atom-bomb blasts had on the soldiers. Human behavior specialists from the Johns Hopkins University Operations Research Office (ORO) also were hired by the Pentagon to study the troops' performance at the atomic maneuver. Their methods of investigation differed distinctly from the HumRRO scientists'.

The Johns Hopkins researchers set out to appraise the performance and psychological reactions of the troops by personally observing the soldiers and listening to their conversations before, during and after the exercise. The ORO team also included a polygraph expert who measured the changes in heart rate and blood pressure among the soldiers at critical points. Dr. John L. Finan, assistant director of HumRRO, was named overall coordinator of the two studies.

While the psychologists carefully prepared the questionnaires and one ORO observer was dispatched to Fort Campbell to spend the last few days before the trip to Camp Desert Rock with the soldiers, AEC Chairman Gordon Dean was squirming under the thumb of Senator McCarran at an appropriations hearing on Capitol Hill. As was always the case when atomic energy matters were involved, the hearing was closed to the public, but some details of the heated exchange between Dean and McCarran did leak out. Because he represented a major mining region, McCarran wanted Dean to divulge exactly how many railroad cars of uranium it took to produce enough of the refined material to make one atomic bomb. Dean was reticent about disclosing the information. The chairman had been warned during a whispering campaign against Mc-Carran that a steady stream of ex-Communists were constantly parading through the senator's Capitol Hill office. The senator, critics charged, couldn't be trusted with sensitive information.

But McCarran still had his trump card to play. And it far outweighed the unfounded allegations that had been spread about him in the back corridors and cloakrooms of Congress. Dean knew that he had to stay in McCarran's good graces to insure that the AEC could continue exploding atomic bombs in the senator's backyard.

Before the hearing was over, Dean relented and answered McCarran's questions. But the chairman balked at revealing the precise number of atomic bombs in the U.S. arsenal when one of the other senators demanded to know the details. That figure remained a secret among President Truman, the AEC commissioners, a few Defense Department planners and Senator Brien McMahon, chairman of the Joint Committee on Atomic Energy.

At AEC headquarters, Dr. Shields Warren was worried about the commission's decision to allow military troopers to maneuver at one of the upcoming Buster-Jangle shots. The Division of Biology and Medicine had authorized a permissible exposure limit of 3.9r of gamma radiation for any period of 13 consecutive weeks — including the test series. But Warren knew that it was ultimately up to Test Director Carroll Tyler to decide whether permission would be granted for "deliberate over-exposures."

To make certain that Tyler knew of his concerns, Warren wrote to him to say that "this Division does not look lightly upon radiation excesses. Only true emergencies should be granted special privileges," Warren continued, "and no upper limit for permissible doses can logically be set for a true emergency."

The doctor also knew that even Tyler couldn't keep the brass hats from making their own decisions about radiological safety, but he made it clear to the test director that requests by the Pentagon to exceed the AEC's safety criteria "will not be granted by this Division."

Warren explained that compliance with the safety guidelines should serve as a "mark of distinction." Indoctrinating the military leaders with that attitude early, he said, "may save us much trouble, and possibly radiation injuries, in the several series to come."

To make the Desert Rock Exercise fit realistically into the physical limitations of the Nevada Test Site, Pentagon planners created an unlikely scenario: Two mythical enemy armies were assumed to have landed on the northwest coast of the United States two months prior to the exercise. Their assault drove the U.S. armies to the southeast. By the end of October, the U.S. Sixth Army was supposedly forced to a line of withdrawal stretching from the West Coast north of Los Angeles through southern Nevada. At that point, the scenario for the war game called for the tactical use of an atomic weapon to force a northward retreat by the enemy, followed by a U.S. counteroffensive.

Early in October, ORO and HumRRO scientists began administering their questionnaires to the paratroopers at Fort Campbell. Though the soldiers never received any official confirmation they would be participating in atomic maneuvers, most of them figured out what their mission was either during the flight to Nevada or shortly after they arrived at the tent encampment called Desert Rock.

Operation Buster-Jangle consisted of seven separate shots — one tower detonation, four airdrops, a surface blast and a crater shot. The explosions ranged from a tenth of a kiloton to 31kt in size. Troops participated in only one of the blasts, code-named Shot Dog, on November 1, 1951.

On D-day, reveille sounded at 2:00 A.M. at Camp Desert Rock. The men were fed and loaded onto trucks for the two-hour, 30-mile ride north to Yucca Flat. They were taken to a point on the desert about seven miles from ground zero. A minute before the blast the soldiers were ordered to "sit down and face south" while the orientation officer continued the countdown over a loudspeaker. The seconds ticked off until the order "Bomb Away" was given at exactly 7:25 A.M.

HumRRO Director Crawford later recalled being amazed by the explicit profanities sprinkling the paratroopers' conversations in the moments before the blast. Though the professor had served in the Army during World War II, the troopers were using expletives he had never even heard before.

About 30 seconds after the detonation, the soldiers were told to turn around so they could watch the fireball after the shock waves passed. One of the most profane of the paratroopers, who moments before was perplexing the professor with his linguistics, seemed to be so taken with the spectacle unfolding before him that he could only manage to utter, "It's extraordinary!"

A half-hour later radiation monitors left to check the levels of activity in the maneuver area. Official observers, including an assortment of generals, nine congressmen and three senators, also boarded trucks and headed for ground zero. But a full hour passed before the troopers were loaded aboard trucks to view the foxholes, ditches and other emplacements they had dug a few days before two miles from the detonation point. The soldiers wandered about, examining the damage and removing the film badge dosimeters that they had left attached to their rifles and other pieces of equipment in the foxholes.

Sandbags on some of the foxholes were badly burned. At one emplacement, pieces of burning burlap had fallen on a rifle, charring the weapon's stock and spontaneously "welding" the rifle's bolt in place so it couldn't be moved. The windshield of a jeep was blown 40 feet behind the vehicle. Fatigues worn by a dummy left in the open were charred. The wool on two sheep left above ground was scorched, and one of the animals, which presumably must have faced the blast, had small burn blisters around its eyes and mouth. A pup tent with a dummy in it was blasted flat, but the dummy itself was apparently none the worse for the experience.

Other emplacements seemed to have suffered no damage at all. The battle tanks in the area were in operable condition. Artillery pieces were undamaged. Nearly all the rifles, machine guns and mortars were where they had been placed and apparently usable. Two more sheep, shielded by foxholes, were calmly eating hay, unruffled by the bomb.

The soldiers were told that if they had been in their foxholes with their backs toward the blast and crouched along the wall nearest the explosion, they would not have been injured. But if they had been above the ground, an estimated 50 percent of them would probably be casualties of the bomb.

After forming into fifteen sticks, the troops began marching closer toward ground zero in single file, each group preceded by an AEC radiation monitor. Between the emplacements two miles from ground zero and a position 1,500 yards from the detonation point, the desert floor was swept clean of loose dust and dirt. Between 1,500 and 500 yards, the ground was blanketed by dust that had been sucked into the vortex of the explosion. At ground zero, vegetation was charred throughout a circle stretching about 500 yards in diameter. Yet at the epicenter of the circle, there was no visible scorching on the desert surface at all.

As they approached to within 500 yards of ground zero, the troops veered off to inspect damage at emplacements encircling the area. Foxholes were caved in. A tank had the rubber on its track burned, its aerial bent and its paint blistered. A jeep, its side facing the blast, had a cracked windshield, discolored headlights and scorched seats, but it was operable. A dummy, left on the surface about 1,000 yards from ground zero, was badly burned. The wool on the rumps and backs of two sheep near the dummy was scorched. One of the animals had a blistered muzzle and one of its eyes blinded. A jackrabbit at 500 yards "appeared dazed," but was able to run off when the soldiers approached.

After a brief examination by radiological monitors, the troops traveled by truck to inspect another area of emplacements four miles south of ground zero. Then it was on to Camp Desert Rock, where they were told to take showers and change clothes. Within a few days, all of the 883 members of the Battalion Combat Team were back at their bases. But the analysis of the data collected by the scientists at Shot Dog was just beginning.

Besides the maneuver troops, 2,786 observers and 1,587 AEC personnel watched Shot Dog, and, though the troops wore no radiation badges, the observers — individuals "who might be exposed to radiation" — were issued dosimeters. At a point 350 yards from ground zero, the radiation levels were measured at one roentgen per hour, an hour after the blast. According to that reading, the troops were not exposed to radiation levels beyond the one roentgen safety limit set by the Army commanders. Unfortunately, because they wore no radiation badges and there was no way to determine whether the troopers breathed alpha or beta particles of radiation, or how long they spent at ground zero, no one will ever know for certain.

Exercises Desert Rock II and III did not involve any maneuvering or observation by troops. However, there were hundreds of weapons effects tests on Army equipment located 100 to 1,000 yards from the various ground zero points. The contamination in the area during those later tests was so heavy the equipment emplacements couldn't be examined until two weeks after the test series was over.

Were the Pentagon generals now able to fill the human behavior factor into the incomplete atomic warfare equation? Yes — and no. Both the HumRRO and ORO researchers dutifully reported their findings in detailed secret reports. But what one group of scientists discovered differed radically from the other.

The HumRRO researchers presented what was basically a very upbeat, positive report — certainly what the brass hats wanted to read. According to the analysis of the soldiers' answers to questions asked both before and after a six-hour indoctrination lecture on atomic effects, their confidence in themselves and the use of the A-bomb "increased materially." Eighty-three percent said they were "not worried at all" about the maneuver, 80 percent said they would volunteer for another similar exercise if they were asked, 78 percent reported they thought the experts really knew enough to use A-bombs in military maneuvers without harming troops and 62 percent indicated they thought they would do "all right" if sent into actual A-bomb combat.

The soldiers' knowledge about the complexities of atomic effects, radiation, flash and blast dangers also increased "substantially" as a result of their thorough indoctrination. Still, some of the men apparently maintained a healthy skepticism in spite of the Army's best propaganda efforts. For example, though the HumRRO researchers reported a "particularly marked" improvement by the troops in their knowledge about radiation, only 48 percent of the soldiers "recognized that it would be safe in ordinary field clothing to move into Ground Zero immediately after an A-bomb burst at 2,000 feet."

After the maneuver, the scientists reported that on no important point did the confidence of the men "decrease materially." In fact, their confidence in themselves and the ability of the experts actually increased. Questions posed by the researchers about psychosomatic complaints such as nervousness or shortness of breath revealed "no significant changes." Of a list of possible adverse physical reactions, in only one instance did any of the troops report any physical effect. The one exception, reported by 18 percent of the men, was trouble with their eyes for a few minutes after the bright flash of the bomb.

The HumRRO researchers undoubtedly pleased their Pentagon bosses when they reported that the initial fears and anxieties of troops about to engage in atomic maneuvers or sent onto an atomic battlefield could "apparently be overcome by indoctrination." But the results of the observations by the ORO psychologists painted a very different picture.

Four groups of data on the behavior of the troops was collected by the Johns Hopkins researchers. By carefully listening to the soldiers talking among themselves and through personal interviews with the troops, the psychologists collected information on "verbal behavior." "Physical behavior" data were obtained both by observation and through polygraph testing.

The scientists reported that the soldiers' responses during private interviews were a much more truthful indication of how they felt about the A-bomb maneuver than the conversations they engaged in with their peers. Likewise, overt physical signs of fright could be hidden from observation, but changes in the soldiers' heart rate and blood pressure couldn't be masked during the lie detector tests.

Before D-day, the ORO researchers reported most of the troopers expressed the view in public and private that "the Army would not risk their safety." Yet among 45 participants interviewed after the blast, "35 claimed that, at the time of the explosion, they had experienced feelings of fright, worry or excitement. Nineteen reported they felt some apprehension about radioactivity when advancing deep into the area of the burst," in spite of assurances that they were safe.

The polygraph examinations disclosed that the soldiers showed "significant physiological disturbance" when they were asked about both real and hypothetical dangers involved in the A-bomb exercise and "more physiological disturbance . . . than their verbal responses indicated."

In other words, even though the soldiers claimed no anxiety about the exercise, their physical reactions belied their brave talk. The researchers also discovered that, though the six-hour A-bomb indoctrination appeared to reassure the troopers on the surface, polygraph exams revealed "significant emotional disturbance" when the soldiers were asked about possible dangers from the bomb.

The psychologists reported no overt signs of fright by the men on D-day itself and noted that all of the troopers performed "adequately."

However, because the paratroopers were all highly motivated volunteers, the ORO researchers cautioned that the performance of more "typical troops" in combat with atomic weapons "cannot be predicted."

After the bomb blast, most of the soldiers' worries and anxieties seemed, for the most part, to disappear. When they were retested on the polygraph machine back at Fort Campbell, their heart rates and blood pressure measurements had returned to normal. A majority of the troopers said they would feel safe, even at positions closer to ground zero — as long as they were in foxholes. Of the 45 participants interviewed at Fort Campbell, 38 said they "would like to have such a weapon as that which they had witnessed to support them in combat."

The Johns Hopkins scientists were quite critical of the "artificiality" of the maneuver. The exercise, they complained, did "not attempt to duplicate a real tactical situation." There was no "enemy" and the "advance" was delayed until radiation levels had been checked. Meanwhile, the troops sat on their duffs and watched "official observers of all kinds preceding them into the 'danger' area." The single-file advance into the maneuver area was "not one which would be used in most combat situations" and the maneuver itself did not present the highly experienced troops "a performance challenge commensurate with their training." The researchers strongly recommended repeating the maneuver "under more realistic conditions."

The brass hats at the Pentagon seemed to be thinking the same thing. In late November, Brigadier General Herbert Loper, director of the Armed Forces Special Weapons Project, wrote to Colonel K. E. Fields of the AEC's Military Application Division to inform him that "the Army has a vital requirement for participation . . . in *all* future atomic tests conducted in the continental United States," if troop movements were feasible. Loper also asked for the AEC's permission to "retain the temporary camp adjacent to the Nevada Test Site."

Within a month, Fields reported to General Loper that the AEC had "no objection" to the semipermanent establishment of Camp Desert Rock. The commission also agreed to allow "limited troop participation" at future tests. Soon after, the Pentagon and the AEC concluded a Memorandum of Agreement, which set forth the responsibilities of each agency and required the Army to keep the commission informed about plans for future operations so security, logistical and technical problems could be ironed out. The exchange of letters was only the beginning of what became a flurry of communications as each agency jockeyed for position and power.

First, Brigadier General A. R. Luedecke, an Air Force officer serving as deputy chief of the Special Weapons Project, asked the AEC for permission to move the soldiers at the next scheduled tests closer to ground zero. Paraphrasing the research reports from the first exercise, Luedecke explained that the Shot Dog maneuver "had some unfavorable psychological effects . . . due to the tactically unrealistic distance of seven miles" from ground zero that the troops were required to occupy. Instead, Luedecke suggested stationing his forces at a "reasonable" distance of 7,000 yards — just under four miles. Luedecke also advised the AEC that the military services "are prepared and desire to accept full responsibility for the safety of all participating troop units and troop observers."

The request by the Army set off a heated debate within the commission. Colonel Fields supported the contentions of his military superiors. He argued that by stationing troops at 7,000 yards, the Army could prove that troops in combat could survive a detonation at that distance and still "emerge immediately thereafter in condition to exploit" the enemy's confusion. To give the commissioners an indication of how strongly the Pentagon planners felt about the issue, Fields told them that "the Marines have stated they would not participate" if they weren't allowed to move closer to the blast.

Carroll Tyler, seeing his bailiwick slowly eroding, reminded the commission that AEC policy prohibited anyone from being within five or six miles of an A-bomb blast. If the Army and the other services insisted on risking their necks, Tyler advised the commissioners to "disclaim all responsibility for injury which might by some remote chance result from their position."

The ever-cautious Shields Warren wasn't ready to give up quite so easily. In a memo to Fields, the health scientist strongly recommended against permitting the troops to be closer to ground zero than seven miles. Warren explained that, though he knew it was not his business to set standards for the military, insuring the safety of tests at the proving grounds *was* his responsibility both "in fact and in the public mind." Warren warned that the public had accepted the Nevada Test Site as safe. Any "accidents" that occurred there would be "magnified by the press out of all proportion to their importance." Besides, the doctor wrote, "the explosion is experimental in type and its yield cannot be predicted accurately."

The dispute came to a head at a meeting of the commission on April 1, 1952. Commissioner Henry Smyth insisted that the Pentagon be advised in no uncertain terms that their suggestions were contrary to AEC safety standards. In the end, the AEC folded under the withering Army attack. The commissioners rationalized caving in to the military's arguments by noting that realistic training was needed in all fields, including the field of atomic weapons. And training that is realistic, they decided, was "often accompanied by serious injuries."

The next day, Chairman Dean wrote to General Loper to give him the good news. Dean explained that the commission agreed with his plans for a troop maneuver with one qualification. He required the military planners to prepare "a safety plan to minimize risk of injury acceptable to the Test Manager." Dean cited the possible hazards to troops stationed 7,000 yards from the bomb, but added "if officials of the Department of Defense . . . still feel that a military requirement justifies the maneuver, the commission would enter no objection."

In the letter to Loper, Dean made one other statement hinting that he and his fellow commissioners were washing their hands of the whole affair. "It is assumed," Dean wrote, "that the monitoring teams will be provided from the troops and that no requirement whatsoever will be placed on the monitoring group of the test organization, since the latter will be otherwise occupied at the time." The radiation dose limit for the exercise was set at three roentgens — a tighter restriction than the AEC workers were required to conform with.

Early in March the first soldiers began arriving in Nevada for Exercise Desert Rock IV. In only six months Camp Desert Rock had grown from a few tents littering the barren desert to a semipermanent base.

The tents themselves were framed and had wooden floors. Several permanent latrines with showers, flush toilets and wash basins replaced the open ditches. There was a post exchange in a small Quonset hut and two mess halls that could each accommodate 500 men at a time. Electric telephone and telegraph wires were strung from Camp Mercury. Water, however, was limited. In spite of the best prospecting efforts by Army engineers, only one well sunk to 1,400 feet struck water. Though it flowed to the surface at a respectable 150 gallons a day, the well water was not fit for drinking. A 100,000-gallon tank provided the camp's only supply of running, potable water.

The psychologists from Johns Hopkins University's Operations Research Office returned to Camp Desert Rock that spring to continue their research into the reactions of troops during atomic maneuvers. Again, they were prepared to administer questionnaires, test the troops with a polygraph and conduct private interviews. This time, however, another phase of research was included. The psychologists planned to test the speed with which a few selected paratroopers could disassemble and reassemble their M–1 rifles. They wanted to know whether witnessing an atomic blast impaired the soldiers' performance.

The HumRRO team was back in action again too. They were continuing their research into how the indoctrination lectures affected the troops' attitudes about atomic weapons. The HumRRO psychologists' methods paralleled their Exercise Desert Rock I research. Questionnaires were administered before the indoctrination lectures, after the lectures and again after the maneuver itself.

The imagined scenario for this test series, called the Tumbler-Snapper, was also similar to the previous test: friendly troops, unable to break through into enemy-held territory, supposedly used an atomic bomb to clear a path through enemy lines. Soldiers, sailors, airmen and Marines either observed or participated in maneuvers at four of the eight shots of the Tumbler-Snapper series.

At the third blast, Shot Charlie, 2,134 soldiers and airmen watched the 31kt airdrop from trenches 7,000 yards away. Twenty-five minutes after the blast, they moved toward ground zero preceded by Army Chemical, Biological and Radiological (CBR) monitors who were being supervised by AEC experts. Nearly two hours after the blast, 200 paratroopers were dropped from the air behind the mythical enemy lines to link up with the soldiers who had advanced through the ground zero area.

The fourth blast, Shot Dog, was primarily a Marine Corps exercise. Two battalions made up of 1,950 Marines from Camp Pendleton, California, and Camp LeJeune, North Carolina, maneuvered through the blast area while 50 other Marines and 100 Navy sailors stayed behind in the trenches after the 19kt bomb was detonated.

At Shot Fox, the sixth of the series, Army CBR monitors were on their own for the first time following the 11kt bomb blast. When the monitors gave the all-clear signal, an armored battalion combat team advanced toward ground zero.

Thirteen hundred troops and 500 observers were involved in the eighth bomb burst of the series — a tower detonation called Shot George. Unlike the previous maneuvers, the battalion combat team began its advance toward ground zero immediately after the burst, without waiting for a radiation safety clearance from either the AEC or the Army CBR monitors. Instead, the troops were led only by poorly trained soldiers who had been assigned to monitoring jobs. Five tanks, crewed by soldiers who had remained in the vehicles during the detonation, led the attack.

After the tests the HumRRO psychologists sent their research results to the Pentagon. The more information the troops had, they reported, the less likely they were to indicate fear during the maneuver. Soldiers with the highest levels of information showed, besides a lower level of fear, a higher confidence about A-bomb combat, a greater willingness to volunteer for A-bomb maneuvers and, interestingly, a more critical attitude toward their life in the Army. Most of the troops claimed they were willing to volunteer to take up positions in foxholes even a mile closer to an A-bomb than they were during the maneuvers.

The results obtained by the ORO researchers didn't differ much from their previous research, with one exception. This time polygraph tests showed that the soldiers were not anxious or tense about the A-bomb. In fact, the tests revealed that the troops were more fearful of ordinary combat dangers than A-bombs. "In all shots," they reported, "there are no indications that troops are seriously disturbed about the dangers of atomic weapons." The researchers also noted that there wasn't even "the slightest evidence" that the atomic explosions caused any impairment in the soldiers' proficiency in disassembling and reassembling their weapons.

The psychologists attributed the change in the polygraph results to the fact that the earlier troops participated in the very first atomic maneuver at Desert Rock I. That made the first exercise "a more stressful experience." Still, the researchers questioned whether the information gained from the Desert Rock IV Exercise justified the nearly $600,000 spent on moving the troops and equipment to and from Camp Desert Rock for the maneuver.

Again, the ORO researchers criticized the maneuvers for "excessive safety precautions" and "unrealistic" training situations. "If reducing the participants' fears of the A-bomb was one of the primary objectives," the psychologists wrote, "then the Desert Rock IV Exercise was of little value," since the maneuvers weren't realistic enough to cause the soldiers to fear anything in the first place. The scientists recommended that future similar maneuvers not be bothered with unless the troops were exposed to conditions "involving danger, surprise, and fatigue approximating those found in combat, or when atomic weapons are actually used in combat operations."

While the test series was underway in Nevada, back in Washington the AEC was beginning to feel the heat from critics who were worried about radioactive fallout from the bomb blasts. "Unusually high fallout" levels near Rochester, New York, sparked concern in that state. Particulate debris from one of the tower shots of the Tumbler-Snapper series blanketed southwestern Utah.

The "conscience of the commission," Dr. Shields Warren, warned at a May meeting to "be careful" to avoid blowing up A-bombs when the winds in the upper atmosphere reached high velocities. Warren also suggested limiting the size of the tower blasts. But as usual the doctor's cautious suggestions were ignored in favor of public relations.

Chairman Dean offered another solution to counter the increasingly unpopular tide of public opinion about the tests. He recommended drafting and planting an article pooh-poohing the fallout dangers in a widely read magazine "to reduce the possibility of public anxiety resulting from a lack of information."

Not long after the Desert Rock IV Exercise, the military planners at the Pentagon picked up the cue about "realism" from their psychologists' reports and began complaining again about the AEC restrictions imposed on their troop movements. The commission didn't stand up well to the pressure. At a meeting of the AEC's Advisory Committee for Biology and Medicine in June, the government health experts agreed that adequate air sampling could not be successfully carried out by the Air Force pilots who flew through the atomic clouds unless "exposure of the order of 20r is received by the pilots."

Air Force planes equipped with sophisticated radiation-monitoring devices regularly flew through the mushroom clouds and tracked the cloud's path across the country. The scientists also decided that since protective clothing would "hamper the success of the mission," they recommended that the pilots continue to "be permitted to receive a dose of 20r with an upper limit of 25r."

In September, Captain John T. Hayward, chief of the Navy's Weapons Research Branch, used the Advisory Committee's action to up the ante once again. In a letter to Dr. John C. Bugher, the new head of the AEC's Division of Biology and Medicine, Hayward asked that even higher limits for radiation exposure for personnel at the AEC tests be set. Hayward noted that "20r has been allowed crews of sampling aircraft without apparent ill effect while the limit for ground personnel has been maintained at 3r." The captain also made certain that Bugher knew the Pentagon chiefs were not too happy with the constraints imposed by the AEC. "Some people in the Department of Defense," Hayward darkly hinted, "have felt the AEC was not realistic in setting present exposure limits."

Planning was already underway at the Pentagon for Exercise Desert Rock V. The brass hats wanted troops to participate in all of the shots of the Upshot-Knothole series scheduled for the following spring. They wanted to upgrade Camp Desert Rock into a permanent Class I installation. The military planners also wanted permission to maneuver more freely, to dig trenches closer to the blast and to double radiation limits to six roentgens — three roentgens of prompt radiation from the bomb and three roentgens of residual radiation during maneuvers.

The AEC was caught in the midst of yet another dilemma. In October, a representative from the AEC Santa Fe office admitted during a meeting of the commission that "exposure problems at the Test Site have not been completely solved." At first there were objections to the Pentagon's plan to double exposure limits, but the protests were decidedly weak. "Our position," the reply to Captain Hayward stated, "is that we probably cannot dictate exposure limits to the military, but we do have the responsibility of informing them of the hazards in order that they may be fully aware of the responsibility which they assume."

To counter that feeble argument, Herbert Loper, by then promoted to the rank of major general, told the AEC that the military services were ready "to accept full responsibility for the physical and radiological safety of troops while in the Nevada Proving Grounds." Loper also promised that if the AEC was criticized about the decision, "the Department of Defense will be prepared to make a public announcement" absolving the commission of any blame.

That was enough for Gordon Dean. He approved the drafting of a press release that read, in part: "The Department of Defense has assumed responsibility for the safety of troops participating in military exercises at the U.S. AEC's Nevada Proving Grounds.

"Military monitoring teams trained by AEC radiation safety monitors at previous tests will govern the movement of troops in the test areas to prevent exposure to harmful radiation. The maximum permissible level of radiation for troops who will participate will be slightly higher than the AEC's standard industrial level . . . [but] is far below that at which any detectable radiation effects have been found in the human body."

At a commission meeting two months later, Dean defended his actions. "Since the Defense Department apparently considered it necessary to conduct the exercise in this manner," he said, "the AEC was not in a position to recommend that the normal limits be observed."

Slowly but surely, the commission abdicated virtually all of its safety and health responsibilities to the Pentagon. And that was a mistake.

3

THE PENTAGON
TAKES CONTROL

After only a muted debate, and without a shot fired in anger, the Pentagon had wrested control over the movement and radiological safety of troops from the hands of the Atomic Energy Commissioners. The commissioners could read the political handwriting on the wall.

Dwight D. Eisenhower, the supreme commander of Allied military forces in Europe during World War II, became the Republican presidential nominee and soundly trounced the Democratic standard-bearer, Adlai Stevenson, in the race for the White House in November 1952. By the grace of conservative southern Democrats, Republicans effectively ruled Congress by the time Ike took office on January 20, 1953.

The polite requests by the Pentagon for new authority at the Nevada Test Site were merely formalities. The AEC glumly succumbed to each of the military's demands. Once merely supplicants to the commission's arbitrary rule, by early 1953 the Pentagon clearly ruled the atomic roost.

In effect, the joint chiefs of staff ganged up on the AEC. The heads of the Army, Navy, Air Force and Marine Corps all wrote the AEC reinforcing the request of General Loper, chief of the Armed Forces Special Weapons Project, for the authority to set safety standards and station troops closer to the atomic-bomb blasts. Only days before Eisenhower's inauguration, M. W. Boyer, the AEC commissioner serving as general manager at the test site, sent Loper a message that made the commission's acquiescence official.

"We accept," Boyer wrote, "the proposal that the Department of Defense assume full responsibility for physical and radiological safety of troops and all observers accompanying troops within the maneuver areas assigned to Exercise Desert Rock V, including suitable safety criteria . . .

The Atomic Energy Commission adopts this position in recognition that doctrine on the tactical use of atomic weapons, as well as the hazards which military personnel are required to undergo during their training, must be evaluated and determined by the Department of Defense.''

Boyer reiterated that the AEC's own criteria for radiological safety would continue to limit its own workers' radiation exposure to 3.9 roentgens for any 13-week period. The test manager informed Loper that ''we consider these limits to be realistic, and further, are of the opinion that when they are exceeded in any operation, that operation may become a hazardous one.''

The Pentagon chiefs virtually ignored Boyer's cautionary warning. They set their own radiological limit for the upcoming Upshot-Knothole test series at six roentgens for any ''one-shot'' training exercise. A month after taking office Eisenhower approved the expenditure of enough of the country's uranium and plutonium resources to detonate ten separate bombs during Exercise Desert Rock V. A few days later the Pentagon strategists began laying plans for their participation in the test series and the Army accepted responsibility for the ''safety of a limited number of correspondents . . . who may be authorized to witness . . . a shot from the trench area where the bulk of the troops will be placed.''

The press correspondents sang a paean to the generals' generosity. Finally, after years of frustration, they were allowed to be firsthand witnesses to the events on Yucca Flat. It wasn't as though the press had been denied a peek at the maneuvers on the desert floor, but rather, they literally had been relegated to the back bleachers by the AEC's penchant for security.

During the early bomb tests in 1950 and 1951, the blasts usually were unannounced. It didn't take long for a few intrepid correspondents to outwit the AEC's efforts at keeping the testing covered with a news blackout.

During Operation Ranger, the AEC set up temporary offices in the El Cortez Hotel in Las Vegas. As the Nevada Test Site operations expanded, the commissioners needed more space for their Las Vegas workers, so a warehouse building at 1235 South Main Street was leased and divided into office spaces. A pole with two lights on it was erected on top of the building. To notify its employees of coming tests, a green light on the pole would be lit. If a test was canceled, a red light shone as a beacon, warning the workers that they need not make the predawn trek to South Main Street to be at their desks and phones in time for the detonation.

Reporters assigned to cover the AEC's Nevada tests soon caught on to the system. Whenever a green light was spotted, the newsmen would make a mad dash out of town toward the test range. The correspondents climbed to the high summit of a mountain known as Angel's Peak, southeast of Frenchman's Flat. Though the peak was outside of the test site itself, and, hence, outside of the AEC's jurisdiction, its cliffs provided a commanding view of the action far below.

Reporters watched the early bomb tests from Angel's Peak and relayed their dispatches back to Las Vegas. But after the tests were moved north to Yucca Flat, the correspondents on Angel's Peak were not just out of luck, they were out of view of everything except the mushroom-shaped clouds that hovered over the desert floor after each blast.

A few selected reporters were invited onto the AEC test site for the first time on April 22, 1952, during the Tumbler-Snapper series. That event also marked the premiere of television coverage of the blasts. The members of the press gathered on a craggy outcropping of basalt rock near the AEC's control bunker and waited. AEC construction worker Tom Sherrod ripped a weatherbeaten board with a door knob attached from an old outdoor privy and painted across it the words "NEWS NOB" in large, yellow letters. By the time of Exercise Desert Rock V the next year, News Nob was a familiar landmark.

The new "open policy" toward the press created some public relations problems for the commission. Word spread quickly that American servicemen were deliberately being exposed to atom-bomb blasts. In short order, a Lexington, Kentucky, woman named Helen Dodds fired off an angry letter to Eisenhower, protesting the use of soldiers at the tests. "When you became President," she wrote, "I thought that the shenanigans about the atomic experiments would be made to conform to the best interests of the country. As a Presbyterian, I know it is downright wicked to experiment with the lives of human beings drafted in peacetime."

Mrs. Dodds also posed an incisive question. "If the men running this experiment say there is no danger, then why," she asked, "do they build such elaborate shelters for themselves, farther away from the explosion area than the troops which have no protection?"

When Eisenhower received the missive from Mrs. Dodds, he reacted in the same way that any long-time military officer steeped in the traditions of the chain of command would react — he gave the letter to his assistant, Sherman Adams, and told him to take care of it. Adams sent it to the Army's surgeon general, who in turn passed the proverbial buck on to the medical officer of the Armed Forces Special Weapons Project for a reply. The answer Mrs. Dodds finally received from Air Force Colonel H. C. Donnelly a month later was both terse and evasive.

"Please let me reassure you," Donnelly began, that "these maneuvers are carried out under conditions of maximum safety, and all troops are amply protected at all times." Without answering the specific questions posed by Mrs. Dodds, the colonel shrugged off her concerns as unfounded. He patronizingly explained that "in none of the many military maneuvers has there been an instance of injury to personnel as a result of exposure to the atomic weapon, and you may rest assured that under present policies, the chances of any such injury in the future are so extremely remote that they are negligible."

Exercise Desert Rock V started off with a bang as a 16kt bomb was detonated atop a 300-foot tower on March 17, 1953. Sensitive dosimeters with a recording range between zero and 10,000 milliroentgens (0–10r) were given to all the VIP guests, each member of the AEC radiation survey teams and each commander of a battalion combat team. One dosimeter with a range between zero and 50,000mr (0–50r) was issued to each platoon leader and the Army's radiation monitors. Individual soldiers had to trust their platoon leaders to tell them when they were in danger.

The troops watched the first blast — Shot Annie — from trenches 3,500 yards away from the steel tower. Fifteen minutes after the bomb was exploded, they jumped from the trenches and "attacked" in the general direction of ground zero, stopping 700 yards short of their objective when radiation levels were judged too hazardous to continue.

Twenty reporters also watched the blast. Some were in the trenches with the troops, the rest at News Nob. During the attack, the clouds of dust in the area turned the Army's planned "controlled advance" into a fiasco. Radiation monitors "lost contact with the troops" and photographers wandered about, unimpeded and unescorted.

At the rest of the Upshot-Knothole blasts, the troops were moved to positions farther away from the bombs. At some tests they stayed in trenches 4,000 yards away. At one blast, they were as far away as 5,000 yards. But "volunteer" officers from the military services were allowed to hunker in trenches as close to three of the bombs as 2,000 yards.

The officers were required to personally compute the effects they would expect to be exposed to in open trenches at various distances from a bomb estimated at 35 to 40kt in size. Among themselves, the volunteers generally decided that 2,000 yards would be a safe distance. The fact that they were so close to the bomb was kept secret from the public and the press.

The day before Shot Simon, the seventh blast of the series, the officers were given thorough physical examinations at the camp dispensary and interviewed by psychologists from HumRRO. Each was issued a lined steel helmet, gas mask, flashlight, canteen and three film badge dosimeters. One dosimeter was taped inside each of their helmets, another was placed in a breast pocket and the third in a hip pocket. Several other metered dosimeters — Geiger counters — were passed out. Cotton was distributed so the men could keep dust out of their ears.

The HumRRO researchers accompanied the officers as far as the main troop positions, 4,000 yards from the projected ground zero. Then the volunteers continued on by truck to a trench dug for them 2,000 yards from the bomb.

The light from the 43kt blast was so intense, the officers later said they couldn't read their survey meters or see anything for at least six seconds. After the shock wave passed over their position, a cloud of "light pebbles and heavy dust" showered the trench.

"The first reading which I was able to obtain on my survey meter," wrote one of the volunteers, Navy Captain Robert Hinners, "was exactly 100 roentgens per hour." The captain reported that within the next ten seconds or so, the needle on his meter moved steadily downward to 50r/hr. The decrease of radiation slowed to a point where it took a full minute for the dose rates to drop to 25r/hr. When Hinners climbed out of the trench, the needle shot back up to 40r/hr. As he walked around the area, surveying the damage, the meter recorded readings as high as 50r/hr again.

The officers stopped to look at some sheep in a nearby shallow trench. They were "singed to a dark brown" on those portions of their bodies that had been exposed to line-of-sight thermal radiation. But the animals were all on their feet and "showed no other evidence of physical injury," Hinners reported. Though the dust was thick, none of the officers put on his gas mask on the quarter-of-a-mile hike south toward waiting trucks. By the time the officers reached the vehicles, their survey meters were recording radiation level readings of only 10r/hr. After they returned to Camp Desert Rock, the HumRRO psychologists interviewed the officers again and dismissed them.

At Desert Rock V, the HumRRO scientists were again collecting data to show how indoctrination lectures affected soldiers' "anxieties about exposure to atomic effects, perception of other troops' anxieties about such exposure, the soldier's confidence in his ability to do well in atomic combat and the soldier's willingness to volunteer for a mission involving exposure to radiological hazards."

As at all the previous exercises, the information was gathered by comparing the troopers' responses to questionnaires administered before and after the atomic exercises. And, as at all the other tests, the scientists found that there was a "considerable increase in the number of men who believed they would do well in A-combat."

The HumRRO psychologists simply reiterated their earlier claim that the indoctrination lectures led to great gains in information by the troopers, plus an improvement in the soldiers' attitudes toward atomic weapons — and the military strategists who assured them that those weapons could be used safely. The psychologists were struck, they reported, by "the equanimity" with which the volunteers "regarded the experience. Little anxiety was expressed about danger of injury." The officers did suggest, however, that "there was little more to be gained by placing volunteer groups in forward positions on future shots, or from stationing large numbers of troops at this distance on future shots."

Brigadier General H. P. Storke, the Camp Desert Rock commander, sent all the troops a personal message. "In this exercise, for the first time in known history," Storke wrote, "troops successfully attacked directly toward ground zero immediately following the atomic explosion. You can remember, with a sense of pleasure and accomplishment, that you were one of those troops, a real pioneer in experimentation of the most vital importance to the security of the United States."

The test series also gave the Pentagon a chance to experiment with "surrogate" soldiers. Pigs, rabbits and sheep were left in the open near the bomb blasts. That way, the soldiers could see what might happen to them if they faced an atomic bomb unprotected by the shielding of trenches and foxholes. In all, there were 78 different military effects tests conducted during the Upshot-Knothole blasts, including the following unlikely incident that has come to be known as the "Charge of the Swine Brigade."

Evidence from the Hiroshima and Nagasaki bomb blasts showed that the clothing worn by residents who weren't in the immediate vicinity of the explosions played a vital role in protecting them from severe burns. The Army wanted to find out which fabrics afforded the most protection. Did the clothing need to be fire resistant? How many layers of fabric were needed? And at what distance from ground zero did the clothing not make any difference at all? To find the answers, several different military uniform fabrics were tested. As their "surrogate" soldiers, the Army researchers used shaved White Chester pigs fitted with specially tailored uniforms.

Several representative porkers were measured by Department of Agriculture experts at a government farm near Beltsville, Maryland. Uniforms were made up in two sizes and fitted to individual pigs on the basis of weight. Seams, zippers and drawstrings on the pigs' uniforms were matched exactly to the specifications of the Army's own standard, GI-issue field jackets. Some of the pigs were even given corporal's and sergeant's stripes. One soldier, a practical joker who worked on the project as an assistant to one of the researchers, pinned a pair of general's stars on the ugliest swine he could find.

The "guinea pigs" were placed on welded iron frames and strapped into place after being anesthetized with a sedative. Fifty-five pigs were exposed at one shot, and 56 at another. As soon as the test area could be safely entered after the blasts, the animals were removed from their holders and taken back to the base. There they were photographed in various stages of undress in both black and white and color. Unfortunately, the experiments weren't entirely satisfactory.

Out of 111 animals, 72 were recovered dead. Certain physiological reactions of the skin occur only if the animals are alive. Many of the results of the pig-exposures were invalidated by the fact that the animals were deceased. However, the Army researchers determined that none of the pigs died solely from burns. Four of the swine closest to ground zero, including the late, lamented General Pig, were "blown apart," according to an Army analysis of the experiment. Two more were killed by ionizing radiation. But the majority of the rest died simply because they were overanesthetized and succumbed to exposure in their weakened state. The Charge of the Swine Brigade turned out to be a massacre. Still, the Army did gain some useful information about the thermal protection properties offered by its uniforms — thanks to the sacrifice of the porcine martyrs.

While the bombs were exploding in Nevada, fireworks were going off at AEC headquarters in Washington. Dr. Bugher of the AEC's Division of Biology and Medicine had only bad news to report. At a tripartite meeting of scientists from the United Kingdom, Canada and the U.S., both the foreign delegations were "unwilling to endorse the standards in effect at the Nevada test site." Apparently, they had good reasons for their refusal to endorse the AEC's standards.

Bugher described the fallout that had rained down after the April 25 detonation, which itself "had considerably exceeded the estimated yield." The doctor explained that in some areas, residents might have received radiation doses "as high as 10 roentgens." Fortunately, Bugher said, "only thinly populated areas had been affected."

The day after the blast, Troy, New York, was the scene of a "sharp rain-out" of radiation with doses in the vicinity of two roentgens. Though Chairman Dean recalled that there had been an unofficial understanding prohibiting the detonation of high-yield weapons within the continental U.S., he reminded the assembled commissioners that "no firm criteria for deciding such issues has been established."

The AEC discussed a proposal for an additional eleventh shot of the Upshot-Knothole series on May 18. Dean said he was "concerned that so large a detonation might produce serious shock in nearby communities or that it might cause severe fallout or rain-out on more distant localities." The commissioners decided that since the extra shot would be the last in the series, they could take special precautions to choose exactly the right weather to minimize any risk.

The next day, one of the regularly scheduled Tumbler-Snapper bombs was detonated and fallout rained down on the town of St. George, Utah. Readings were as high as six roentgens and the frightened townspeople were advised to remain indoors from nine o'clock in the morning until noon that day.

The fallout was a prominent topic of conversation when the commissioners met again on Thursday, May 21. They called Test Manager Graves to Washington to explain exactly which criteria were considered before a decision was made to fire a bomb off. Graves told them that shots were not fired if winds at the 30,000-to-45,000-foot altitude were blowing in the direction of St. George or Las Vegas. Shots also were postponed, he explained, if rain was forecast within the area.

Commissioner M. W. Boyer bluntly asked Graves whether "the fact that the test organization is under pressure to meet the test schedule makes them more apt to take chances when they are running behind." "No chances are taken," replied Graves insistently, "in order to meet the schedule." Dean ordered Graves to make sure that he conveyed the commission's concern that "everything be done to avoid another fallout over St. George."

One participant in the meeting, recently promoted Brigadier General K. E. Fields, seemed almost deaf to the worried discussion about fallout in Nevada. He interrupted Dean to remind the chairman that if the eleventh shot at the test site was going to be fired, an announcement had to be made. Eugene Zuckert, one of the more cautious members of the board, refused to be rushed to a decision by the general. He told his fellow commissioners that the fallout incident at St. George, the claims of livestock deaths near the test site and allegations that the bomb blasts were adversely affecting weather conditions "makes me fear the effect of testing a device at Nevada considerably larger than any previously fired there."

"A serious psychological problem has arisen," Zuckert declared, "and the AEC must be prepared to study an alternate to holding future tests at the Nevada Test Site. In the present frame of mind of the public, it would take only a single illogical and unforeseeable accident to preclude holding any future tests in the U.S."

Commissioner Smyth wasn't quite convinced the blast would be dangerous, since the test could be delayed until weather conditions were perfect. But Smyth agreed with Zuckert's concern about the "public relations aspects of the tests." Zuckert pointed out that though Eisenhower had already approved a routine request for the fissionable material necessary for the eleventh bomb, "the request did not inform him of the magnitude of the shot or the possible dangers involved." Zuckert suggested telling Ike's new special assistant on atomic energy, Lewis Strauss, about the possible problems that could crop up with the eleventh blast.

"Zuckert is very unhappy over it [the eleventh shot] in terms of public relations," Dean wrote in his personal diary later that day. But the commissioner noted for posterity that he told his fellow commissioners that the test was "so important, we will have to go ahead. We just have to take a chance."

According to the diary, Strauss called Dean the following Monday and left him a message. "Assuming that it will not take as long as I was told to set the test up for the 'picnic grounds' [Eniwetok] and that the maximum delay would be of the order say of a month and a half, would it not be better," Strauss reportedly asked, "to accept that, rather than run the risk of a situation which might make all future continental tests impossible?"

Dean's diary also records a telephone conversation the two men had the next day discussing the merits of the eleventh shot. "I think on evaluation," Dean said, "you will find this less risky than ones we have shot before because of the energy release." Dean told Strauss that Eniwetok posed certain problems. "Some aircraft cannot be flown there," Dean argued, "and a two-month delay would be too late." "I see what you mean," Strauss replied, and promised Dean that he would "get to him [Eisenhower] and get an answer if I can."

Strauss called Dean again on May 27 to tell him that Eisenhower had approved the extra test. The chairman immediately passed on the news to his public relations expert, Morse Salisbury, along with some added instructions. According to his diary, Dean advised the P.R. man that in the meeting with Strauss that morning, "the President expressed some concern, not too serious, but made the suggestion that we leave 'thermonuclear' out of our press releases and speeches. Also 'fusion' and 'hydrogen'. The President says," Dean told Salisbury, "keep them confused as to 'fission' and 'fusion.' "

Apparently, the unscheduled eleventh shot of the Upshot-Knothole series might have been a test of one of the nation's first workable hydrogen bombs. The exact yield and type of the bomb was never listed on the government's official compilation of "announced nuclear tests." Whether Eisenhower wanted to confuse the Russians or the American people about the nature of the bomb is unclear. Strauss, Dean and Eisenhower all took the answer to that question with them to their graves.

The natives in the regions surrounding the Nevada Test Site were becoming restless. The bomb blasts were blamed for everything from changes in weather patterns to the death of sheep and cattle grazing on nearby lands. In one case, several cattle in a field near Charleston Peak were reported to have died from radiation poisoning. Veterinarians from the Nevada state government and AEC experts were dispatched to the scene. They determined that the cattle died from malnutrition, not radioactivity. But claims from disgruntled ranchers continued to pour in.

Several horses grazing in the region known as Papoose Valley, eight miles from the test site, had beta radiation burns on their skin. Six cattle, which witnesses saw drinking from a water hole in the valley, died a day after they quenched their thirst.

AEC monitors reported that the water had less than a maximum permissible dose concentration of radioactivity in it. Dell and Cornell Stewart, two brothers who owned grazing rights in Papoose Valley, demanded that the AEC buy their burned horses. Dan Sheahan, the owner of Groom Mine, also wanted the government to buy him out because he had to constantly shut down his operation every time a bomb was detonated south of his mine. The AEC sent representatives to Nevada for meetings with the claimants.

The AEC presented elaborate briefings full of graphs and charts explaining radioactive fallout pathways and their effects. By confounding the livestockmen and miners with scientific jargon and reassuring platitudes, the government effectively defused the protests — at least temporarily — by promising to look into the evidence and review the claims. But the credibility gap between the government and the residents of outlying areas near the test site was widening. In Washington, AEC staff member Dr. Gordon Dunning announced at a commission meeting that the "people of the vicinity of the Nevada Proving Ground no longer have faith in the AEC."

Morse Salisbury began preparing a new public relations assault. The Division of Biology and Medicine was ordered to begin an analysis of fallout problems for the commission's annual report to Congress. Before the report was released, the AEC planned to call public meetings in St. George and Salt Lake City so residents could be treated to the government's official interpretation of the questions raised about fallout. A film on the tests, already prepared but never released, was re-cast and extra footage was shot in the St. George area so nervous viewers from the region could see familiar faces on the screen decrying any danger. As an extra hedge against the growing public disillusionment with the AEC, the film's premiere tentatively was scheduled in St. George.

After exhaustive biological tests, the evidence pointed to the inescapable conclusion that the horses in Papoose Valley had indeed suffered beta burns from test fallout. The cause of the deaths of several hundred sheep had not, however, been so clearly established. The manager of the Santa Fe Operations Office was instructed to negotiate with the animals' owners to settle their claims.

In most cases, the AEC refused to buy the livestockmen's assertion that their sheep and cattle had been felled by radiation. The AEC apparently would admit responsibility only for injuries that could be seen. The beta burns on the Stewart horses couldn't be denied, and so the Stewarts were paid off. But the claims for radiation poisoning of cattle and sheep were not honored.

The AEC's Seth Woodruff flatly told the ranchers that "we can keep no one from putting in a claim," but warned them they probably would be wasting their time and money. "On the basis of our tests, there was no damage," he said. "You could bring suit, but the AEC has no authority for paying more than one thousand dollars [per claim]."

Early in July 1953, Lewis Strauss left his White House advisory post to return to the Atomic Energy Commission. This time, he returned not as a minority Republican member of an organization dominated by Democrats, but as the chairman, appointed to a five-year term by Eisenhower. He inherited not only a well-oiled, growing bureaucratic machine, but also the problem that had come to plague the commission — fallout. Strauss raised the issue at the first meeting he chaired.

"Dr. Shields Warren tells me," Strauss said, "he is concerned that the commission might have underestimated the seriousness of the fallout problem."

"That's not true," Commissioner Henry Smyth responded defensively. "There has been no disposition on the part of the commission to think that the problem was not a most serious one."

To allay public fears, Smyth suggested including in the report to Congress scheduled for release later that month a new table showing that the level of radiation exposure from atomic test fallout was similar to the exposure one would get from normal medical X-rays. Strauss and the other commissioners eagerly accepted the suggestion.

The medical X-ray comparison was an often-used ploy on the part of the AEC to convince the public that fallout was harmless. It's an argument that is still used today whenever a nuclear power plant blows a gasket and spews radiation into the air or water. Unfortunately, the analogy is severely faulted.

First of all, medical X-rays are to be avoided if possible. In fact, the medical community has come under increasing pressure to avoid the possible risk of radiation injury from unnecessary X-rays. But second, and even more important, is the fact that the use of medical X-rays in diagnosis and treatment of some disease can have significant benefits. In contrast, there are no benefits from fallout that make the risk worthwhile.

Lacking that subtle distinction, the X-ray fallout comparison was used widely, and effectively, by the AEC to dispel public concern. Shortly after his arrival at the commission, Strauss initiated a hard-line approach. He knew that by carefully limiting the type and flow of information to the public, he could also help insure that nothing interfered with the AEC's Nevada testing program.

Strauss was the antithesis of his predecessor, Gordon Dean. While Dean was introspective and analytical, Strauss was headstrong and forceful. Dean was open to the suggestions and counsel of the commissioners. Strauss listened, but was fond of giving orders on courses of action that many believed he had decided upon long before consulting with the rest of the commission. For example, Commissioner Thomas Murray was the first at the AEC to publicly warn of the danger of strontium 90 radiation from fallout. When he went to New York early in 1954 to make a public speech, Strauss ordered another commissioner, Dr. Willard Libby, to issue a statement refuting Murray, even before the speech was given.

A bit vain, Strauss often climbed upon a stack of thick books for official portraits so his small stature would be hidden from the camera's eye. Fifty-seven years old when he became AEC chairman, Strauss insisted that all his subordinates pronounce his name "straws." He also demanded absolute loyalty, not only on the part of the other commissioners, but the AEC staff as well. Only five days after being sworn in as chairman, Strauss also showed another trait of his character — vindictiveness. The object of the admiral's wrath was Dr. J. Robert Oppenheimer.

Years earlier, AEC Chairman David Lilienthal had been accused at Senate hearings of "incredible mismanagement" during his tenure at the commission. At the time, Strauss, then an AEC commissioner, testified that Lilienthal's decision to export radioactive isotopes for medical research might help some European power produce atomic weapons. His testimony on the witness stand was followed by Oppenheimer's, which completely demolished the admiral's argument and made him look like a fool. Strauss never forgave "Oppie" for the insult.

Early in May 1953, Wisconsin's Senator Joe McCarthy considered going after Oppenheimer during an anti-Communist crusade. But McCarthy's advisers warned him that the scientist's record was well known. Oppenheimer's tenuous connection with Communists had been thoroughly probed by the House Un-American Activities Committee when Richard Nixon was still a congressman. The scientist was completely cleared of suspicion. McCarthy's aides wisely advised him that another investigation of Oppenheimer was bound to backfire. Only two months later, Strauss picked up the gauntlet.

Immediately after assuming the reins of the AEC, Strauss appointed David "Fatty" Teeple to be his special assistant. A close friend of McCarthy's assistant, Don Surine, Teeple had worked for the Joint Committee on Atomic Energy when that organization was probing the AEC. Teeple was considered a link between McCarthy and Strauss. The chairman quickly ordered Teeple to reopen the Oppenheimer investigation.

Failing to dig up any new facts on the case, Strauss asked Oppenheimer to come and see him December 21, 1953. "Someone," said Strauss to the astonished scientist, "has revived these old charges against you." The admiral urged Oppenheimer to resign his government job, but the physicist resisted the blunt pressures by the new chairman.

Two days later Oppenheimer handed Strauss a letter stating that he couldn't possibly resign in the face of the absurd charges made against him and that he fully intended to fight it out. In reply, Strauss handed Oppenheimer a letter of suspension.

Oppenheimer quickly asked the AEC for formal hearings. Though Strauss had discussed the matter with Eisenhower and convinced the President that a security review of Oppie was a good idea, the chairman was worried about the public reaction to the mock trial if details leaked out. As expected, a leak did occur — to Senator McCarthy. The Wisconsin demagogue seized upon Oppenheimer's suspension to buttress his groundless charges that spies had been involved in the atomic-bomb development program. Oppenheimer eventually was hounded out of the government, even though he was innocent of any wrongdoing.

Top scientists in the government began resigning in droves. They resented the admiral's highhanded rule at the AEC. "History will record," remarked one dejected scientist, "that the American people are paying a terrible price for the Strauss ego."

Strauss himself worried about the resignations. But like a captain whose crew has jumped overboard, the bail-out by the scientists only renewed Strauss's resolve to make his control over the commission complete. He imposed a total news blackout on the organization, forbidding his fellow commissioners from talking to the press or making speeches.

In the months following Strauss's ascension, fallout soon became an important factor, in fact, the overriding factor, in many of the commission's actions. At an AEC meeting in October 1954, Dr. William E. Ogle of the AEC's Los Alamos Laboratory summarized the situation. "In the past," he said, "we have let other things other than fallout affect our decision as to whether or not to fire a shot. We have been under some pressures having to do with the importance of the shot — the fact that we had large numbers of VIPs, something of this sort — and it is clear that this sort of thing cannot be allowed to affect our decisions in the future."

Pointing to St. George on a map, Dr. Ogle insisted that "we should not put any large, single dose [of fallout] onto those people again." Indicating northern Nevada, he continued his argument, saying, "There is practically nothing up here. These are mines. These people are very good at getting under cover when we warn them when we go out there. There is very little until you get to Ely, so it is easy to protect this sort of thing. We must worry about this valley that comes down here — St. George, Overton and Las Vegas. We must and will operate with the attitude that we do not have to fire a shot tomorrow, it can wait until next week, and we will sit there until the weather is proper."

Damned if they did, and damned if they didn't, the AEC's new policy of letting weather and fallout patterns determine shot schedules quickly led to problems. Plans were approved late in October for 14 more shots at the Nevada Test Site. The series was code-named Operation Teapot, and Exercise Desert Rock VI was scheduled to coincide with it. The Defense Department again accepted responsibility for the radiological safety of troops who were to participate only during the blasts of high-yield bombs.

The test series began on February 18, 1955, with the explosion of a one-kiloton device dropped from the air. Military observers were restricted to News Nob, more than five miles away. During the subsequent shots, the troops watched from trenches as close as 2,500 yards and as far away as five miles. Some soldiers were permitted to sit in tanks and armored personnel carriers during the blasts and then approach ground zero in their vehicles. At one test, readings as high as 12 roentgens were reported in the tanks. But compared to the earlier exercises, Desert Rock VI was a picnic.

The official Marine Corps critique of the exercise was blunt. "It is considered," read the leathernecks' report, "that the artificialities necessary because of the restrictions imposed in an operation of this type precluded full pursuit of the objective of further evaluating and developing tactics and techniques involved in the execution of air-ground task force missions when atomic weapons are employed." In all, only 8,185 soldiers, airmen and Marines participated in the 14 shots of Desert Rock VI.

It was early in the test series that the AEC's decision to be more careful about fallout led to a problem. New Mexico Senator Clint Anderson, new chairman of the Joint Committee on Atomic Energy, went to Nevada to watch a shot. During other tests, if a visitor of Anderson's stature was at the test site, the bombs were fired rain or shine. But this time, the scheduled blast was delayed. And delayed again. Meanwhile, Anderson was being roused early each morning to prepare for a detonation that never occurred. Fed up with the delays after a week, the senator returned to Washington in a huff.

It wasn't generally known outside the circles of government, but a hot feud was brewing between Strauss and Senator Anderson. The New Mexico senator was a quiet, reflective legislator who resented Strauss's insistence on keeping his plans secret from the congressional watchdog committee. Muckraker Drew Pearson reported in his nationally syndicated column that "the two men are so incensed at each other, the atmosphere fairly crackles when they meet. They are no longer on speaking terms, except when officially necessary. They communicate by mail." But even Strauss was unprepared for the angry letter he received from Anderson after the senator returned to Washington.

"Experience so far in the present series," Anderson wrote, "prompts me to raise the question of whether the Nevada Test Site can be utilized effectively and economically under the present criteria for anything other than very small yield devices.

"The test site was established primarily so that the weapons development laboratories could field-test experimental devices easily and quickly. It was argued that the use of a continental test site, rather than one in far Pacific, would provide savings in money and more importantly, in time of key scientists and would interfere as little as possible with normal laboratory operations. Already we have seen in the present series a delay of one week, and unless I am mistaken in my interpretation of the criteria under which the test organization presently operates and the commitments given the public, we shall see much more costly delays. One weather scientist informed me that the probability of finding weather conditions that meet all present criteria is about one day in twenty-five.

"I would appreciate receiving from the commission an evaluation of the Nevada Test Site under the present criteria for test operations. Your report should consider whether only very small yield devices should be tested there, leaving all substantial shots for the Pacific, where they can be precisely scheduled.

"Please do not misunderstand me," Anderson chided, "I do not advocate taking any real risk with public health and safety; rather, assuming that the present criteria are necessary for public safety, I am raising the question of whether we can use the Nevada Test Site efficiently for anything other than the test of very small yield devices."

Anderson's message to the commission was clear: determine whether the strict criteria governing weather was really necessary to preclude dangerous fallout. If it was, then be prepared to accept an end to high-yield testing in Nevada. The letter from the powerful senator touched off an anxious discussion at the AEC's meeting of February 23, 1955. Strauss was astounded by Anderson's ultimatum, but at the same time he was certain that the senator's momentary disgust with the delays in Nevada could be assuaged.

"There is a Nevada legislator," Strauss reported optimistically, "who has introduced a bill in the legislature, asking us to move out of the state. Both of the Las Vegas papers, which seldom agree on anything, published editorials agreeing that this was nonsense, that we brought a lot of prosperity to the state. This was a fine thing for national defense and they rather laughed this fellow out of court."

"That is a sensible view," seconded AEC commissioner Dr. Willard Libby. "People have got to learn to live with the facts of life, and part of the facts of life are fallout."

"We must not let anything interfere with this series of tests — nothing!" Commissioner Thomas Murray was adamant.

"I think this should be answered promptly," Strauss announced. "He should be told as far as the scheduling is concerned, he speaks of the week's delay, we delayed the second shot in the Pacific, although much larger, for two or three weeks."

"Our whole program contemplated delay," interjected Commissioner K. D. Nichols. "That was the way it was set up."

"It really worked them up very much," lamented Strauss, forlornly, "to get out there on a scheduled day — you know how these things are, there is a weather conference and another one three hours later, and nobody knows whether to go to bed or not. It is very irksome. We could not stage it for them. They just turned around and left."

"Just say we are glad to get his letter," suggested Murray. "Tell him we are taking more precautions and more than we have in the past. It may take a longer time to run the series, we will look into it. We recognize the difficulties and we will look into another site."

A letter was drafted to Anderson in an attempt to mollify the irritated senator. A few days later a 43-kiloton bomb was exploded in Nevada, even though the commission had been warned that the detonation might involve "a slight fallout, well within the safety criteria, in the area of St. George." The cumulative dose limit for the Teapot series was set at 3.9r. The day before the 43kt blast, the commission had discussed the advisability of going ahead with it.

"I have forgotten," said Strauss, "the number of people at St. George."

"Forty-five hundred," he was told.

"So you cannot evacuate them?" Strauss wondered.

"No, you can't," came the reply.

"St. George is hypertensified," commented Dr. John Bugher wanly. "It is not a question of health and safety with St. George, but a question of public relations."

After Upshot-Knothole, southern Utah was considered a forbidden zone for fallout. But the pressure from Capitol Hill quickly led to a reevaluation. The best-laid plans were tossed out the window, and St. George became a fallout target once again. It was either that or face banishment to the South Pacific. It wasn't hard for the commissioners to choose the easy way out of the dilemma.

The Teapot series continued. To deal with the "public relations" questions cited by Bugher, a Health and Safety Fact Sheet was prepared and disseminated in areas near the test site. In addition, Strauss personally recommended that "a list of rumors regarding fallout from weapons tests be prepared as a basis for a possible public release rebutting these rumors." Though the chairman was anxious to deal with possible adverse public reactions, he wasn't ready to face the real issue — fallout.

Even though there is little annual precipitation in Nevada, spring is considered the "rainy season." The Teapot series coincided with the annual rains. The storms, of course, simply increased the fallout in nearby areas. High winds in the upper atmosphere carried the rest of the radioactive debris to the far corners of the nation.

When Val Peterson, head of the Federal Civil Defense Administration, recommended that the AEC cough up $50,000 to pay for a Weather Bureau fallout monitoring program, Strauss was incensed. If Peterson was so worried about fallout, Strauss insisted, then let his budget-strained agency pay for the study. Peterson replied that because the AEC was exploding atomic bombs and causing fallout, the commission should pay. But Strauss steadfastly refused to authorize the expenditure, and the study was never undertaken.

By May 5, the Teapot series was over. The following year, 1956, the AEC moved its testing operation to Eniwetok and Bikini in the Pacific. The move was not governed predominantly by concerns of fallout, but rather because the 18 bombs exploded on the quiet Pacific atolls included several hydrogen bombs. Strauss himself had proudly told the nation that these thermonuclear devices could destroy any city on earth. To test the H-bomb in Nevada with troops nearby was considered just too dangerous.

In November 1956, Eisenhower was reelected to the presidency in a landslide victory over his old adversary — Adlai Stevenson. A month after Ike's second inaugural, in January 1957, the AEC began laying plans for a triumphant return to testing in Nevada that summer.

The 1957 series was code-named Operation Plumbbob. Preliminary arrangements called for military maneuvers on a grander scale than ever before. There would be helicopter assaults and bombs as big as 80 kilotons. It was to be a test series of epic proportions. And among the bit players in the epic were Russell Jack Dann and the other paratroopers from the 82nd Airborne Division making up Task Force Big Bang.

4

MUSHROOM CLOUDS
OVER NEVADA

Nevada was noticeably colder when the government's atomic scientists returned to the state in the spring of 1957 after a year of bomb testing in the Pacific. The mean temperature didn't really vary much from the previous year, but the mood of many residents of the southwest had changed dramatically. There was no abrupt turnabout in attitude toward the atmospheric bomb testing program. Yet a slow metamorphosis was underway.

Catalyst of the change was knowledge. The cloak of secrecy surrounding the bomb testing was being punched full of holes. Scientists outside of government were closely questioning the AEC's confident claims of absolute safety. Mounting evidence indicated that the government had been less than truthful about possible risks from radioactive fallout.

In the early years, AEC technicians in Nevada were greeted warmly as they made their appointed rounds. By 1957, they were hailed with only perfunctory courtesy, and, often, suspicion. The scientists were viewed as unwanted interlopers, whose presence was seen as a nuisance fraught with danger.

Groom Mine owner Dan Sheahan had gladly opened his home to the scientists in 1951. One AEC staffer was allowed to write in Sheahan's diary: "We don't know whether we have become honorary members of the Sheahan family," the inscription read, "or whether the Sheahans are honorary members of the AEC."

Whatever the case, within a couple of years the Sheahans no longer considered it any sort of honor to be neighbors of the Nevada Test Site. The unannounced explosions often shook the miner's home to its rafters and he sued the government for damages. Warnings of high radiation by the AEC forced the closure of Groom Mine regularly. Sheahan's wife also sued the AEC. She charged that mysterious burns which had appeared on her face were caused by fallout. In 1957, the relationship between the Sheahans and the AEC was far from friendly.

Two years earlier, at a ranch a hundred miles north of the test site, seven-year-old Martin Bardoli had eagerly awaited each bomb blast during the 1955 series. For "Butch," as the tow-headed youngster was known, the explosions were a magnificent show. The boy exulted with wonder when the mushroom clouds rose high into the sky. But Butch Bardoli wasn't around to watch the continuation of the pyrotechnic displays in 1957. He had died in a Reno hospital the year before — a victim of leukemia. His mother, Martha, was convinced that her son had been stricken by radioactive fallout. She was not alone in her conviction.

Thousands of people were feeling the belated effects of the bomb blasts throughout Nevada, Utah and Arizona. Residents who lived in the path of the fallout clouds found that their hair fell out and burns inexplicably appeared on exposed portions of their bodies weeks after the clouds flew by. Wells and cisterns were contaminated with white ash and small beadlike particles — the remains of atomized steel detonating towers. Livestock died by the hundreds and thousands. All of these events and incidents helped fuel a burgeoning antinuclear movement across the country.

Responding to the growing public disenchantment with the atom-bomb tests, the Joint Committee on Atomic Energy held hearings in the spring of 1957 on fallout. Under the gun, the AEC trotted out its top experts to befuddle the committee with convoluted and complex scientific arguments minimizing the danger.

The government's witnesses went to extremes to gloss over their own bungling and miscalculations in an attempt to avoid any blame. Showing incredible gullibility, the committee allowed most of the AEC's assertions to go unchallenged and the hearings were recessed with many critical questions unanswered. The legislators assumed that by forcing the issue into a public forum for debate, they had discharged their responsibility. The fact that the debate was decidedly one-sided apparently didn't faze most of the congressmen.

The public backlash over fallout created great consternation and hand-wringing at AEC headquarters in Washington. The hearings before the

Joint Committee marked only a temporary ebb of the fallout furor, and AEC officials were understandably worried about the fuss. Their reaction was predictable — in March, the AEC kicked off a massive public relations campaign to mute opposition to the testing.

Six films were prepared in anticipation of the upcoming Plumbbob series to present the government's own explanations of the testing and fallout danger. Three films — *A Is for Atom, Atomic Energy* and *Atomic Tests in Nevada* — were most prominently exhibited.

Film showings were hosted across the nation by specialists hired by the AEC and assigned to the Off-Site Radiological Safety Organization (RAD-SAFE). These specialists were students, teachers, college professors, public health officials, scientists and proponents of atomic energy from private industry. Though some background in public health issues was a desirable quality in the RAD-SAFE staff, the only real qualification that seemed necessary was a loyal conviction in the work of the AEC.

The RAD-SAFE specialists crisscrossed the countryside, spreading the atomic gospel according to Lewis Strauss. No potential audience of converts was considered too small. With missionary zeal, presentations were made to high school and junior high school pupils. Science classes and Boy Scout troops were favored audiences. The "missionaries" visited 4–H clubs, county fairs, women's clubs, Lion's and Elk's clubs. Even elementary school students and inmates at state penitentiaries were targets of the propaganda campaign.

According to the Plumbbob Off-Site Rad-Safety report written a year after the tests concluded, the importance of an effective public relations assault for the 1957 series was recognized early. "There are many similarities," the report explains, "between 'selling' continental weapons tests with their resultant fallout and 'selling' a milk-control or mosquito abatement program. The major difference in such activities is one of terminology."

The AEC published and distributed 30,000 copies of a small green pamphlet entitled "Atomic Tests in Nevada," designed to convince nervous neighbors of the test site that the bomb blasts were benign. The pamphlet, chock-full of misleading and inaccurate information, should be written in the annals of social psychology as a hallmark in government attempts to propagandize the populace.

"You people who live near the Nevada Test Site," the pamphlet began, "are in a very real sense active participants in the Nation's atomic test program. You have been close observers of tests which have contributed greatly to building the defenses of our country and of the free world. Nevada tests have helped us make great progress in a few years, and have been a vital factor in maintaining the peace of the world."

The pamphlet went on to explain that, though some residents near the test site had been "inconvenienced" by the operations, "to our knowledge no one outside the test site has been hurt in six years of testing. Only one person, a test participant, has been injured seriously as a result of the 45 detonations. His was an eye injury from the flash of light received at a point relatively near ground zero inside the test site. Experience has proved the adequacy of the safeguards which govern Nevada test operations."

The brochure also summarized the AEC's experience with fallout and quickly dismissed any fear as unfounded. *"Simply stated,"* the pamphlet noted, "all such findings have confirmed that Nevada test fallout has not caused illness or injured the health of anyone living near the test site."

Most of the Southwesterners had heard similar assurances before. Some nonbelievers invested in costly Geiger counters to measure radioactive fallout on their homes and property. It was common for AEC technicians to encounter a lone shepherd on a remote range with one of the instruments strapped to his horse's saddle. The gadgets posed yet another problem for the AEC propagandists to address. Here were ordinary citizens armed with sophisticated radiation monitors, eager for the chance to catch the government in a lie. The AEC felt compelled to discredit any challenges to its veracity. The propaganda effort rose to the challenge.

"Many persons in Nevada, Utah, Arizona and California have Geiger counters these days," the pamphlet explained. "We can expect many reports that 'Geiger counters are going crazy today.' Reports like this may worry people unnecessarily. Don't let them bother you. A Geiger counter can go completely off-scale in fallout which is far from hazardous."

Besides the films and pamphlets, AEC workers also gave talks on the off-site monitoring program, set up displays at county fairs, appeared on radio and television and planted favorable articles in newspapers and national periodicals. A group of ranchers and their families was even invited to visit the test site to watch a detonation from the forward observation point. Though the AEC's high-pressure public relations campaign was impressive, it wasn't enough to stifle all the criticism.

Journalist Paul Jacobs published an article in the May 16, 1957, issue of *The Reporter,* warning of the upcoming Plumbbob series and its fallout threat. Jacobs also detailed the lies and half-truths circulated by the AEC and linked the bomb fallout with the death of Butch Bardoli. Soon after, in an editorial that cited *The Reporter* article, the *Christian Science Monitor* called for a "fresh look" at the possibility of banning bomb tests.

Meanwhile, in interviews with reporters, AEC Commissioner Dr. Willard Libby calmly reiterated the AEC's position on fallout danger from the bomb tests. Libby insisted that strontium 90 from the blasts was carried high into the stratosphere and distributed equally around the world. The radioactive substance, Dr. Libby explained, fell "uniformly" to earth. Because the fallout was spread over the globe, there was little danger of large amounts of radiation depositing in any one spot.

Unfortunately for Libby, a survey of strontium 90 in soil samples collected in October 1956 by the U.S. Weather Bureau proved his claims false. In contrast to Libby's assertion of "uniform" deposition, the soil surveys showed that some areas were blanketed with much heavier amounts of fallout than others. Specifically, the rich farmlands of the Midwest seemed to have the highest concentrations of strontium 90 in the soil. The radiation pathways to man were easy to follow.

Radioactive strontium 90 sprinkled the prairies and grasslands where cows grazed. When humans drank the milk from the cows, the strontium 90 was ingested and concentrated in their bones and teeth forever. In St. Louis, a citizens group known as the Committee for Nuclear Information began a Baby Tooth Survey at the suggestion of a Harvard biochemist named Dr. Herman Kalckar. Their plan was to collect information on the absorption of strontium 90 by children. When they found high concentrations of the substance in children's teeth, the results were hailed as a clarion call of danger.

The National Congress of Parents and Teachers quickly approved a resolution calling for an international agreement to end the testing and use of nuclear bombs. Nobel Prize–winning chemist Dr. Linus Pauling, who was the first to cite the danger of radioactive carbon 14 as another fallout hazard, led a group of 2,000 prominent scientists in calling for an end to the testing. "Each added amount of radiation," the scientists warned, "causes damage to the health of human beings all over the world and causes damage to the pool of human gene-plasma such as to lead to an increase in the number of seriously defective children that will be born in future generations."

Pauling was excoriated by the AEC for his trouble. The professor was hard at work on a research project funded by the Department of Health, Education and Welfare. When he signed a petition calling for a test ban, then-HEW Secretary Oveta Culp Hobby abruptly stopped Pauling's research. She even tried to maneuver the California Institute of Technology into continuing the work without Pauling. Luckily, the National Science Foundation made certain that Pauling's research was continued, and eventually Hobby's successor, Marion Folsom, reinstated Pauling's government funding.

Though Pauling's warning went unheeded, it did not go unnoticed. During the 1956 election, Adlai Stevenson made the issue of fallout and weapons testing a political issue for the first time. Concurrently, studies of the atom-bomb survivors from Hiroshima and Nagasaki began to indicate a marked excess of leukemia among the Japanese who lived through the bombings.

Cal Tech professor E. B. Lewis surmised that the studies of the Japanese survivors could foretell worse to come. He published a paper in *Science* magazine, theorizing that the radiation from fallout also could lead to increased leukemia rates in the United States. Pauling went a step further. He extrapolated the leukemia data from Japan down to the doses received by Americans from fallout and predicted a rash of cancers, leukemias and genetic injuries. Pauling assumed there was a linear relationship between the dose and its expected effect.

Dr. Pauling's assertion, and the fact that thousands of scientists agreed with him, placed the AEC's bomb testing program in great jeopardy. Libby's refutations of danger were incredible. Frantic, the AEC commissioners turned to their legion of scientists working at government labs to discredit Pauling and the others.

Ernest Lawrence, head of the government's Livermore, California, laboratory was anxious to help.* He felt that he, and his lab, were in double jeopardy. The Livermore facility was under the academic umbrella of the University of California. Lawrence feared that the university

*The laboratory was later named for Lawrence.

regents might not look kindly upon the fact that they were, through Livermore and the Los Alamos lab, in effect sponsoring the entire weapons testing program.

Lawrence paid a visit to his brother, John, who was head of yet another government research facility, the Donner Laboratory, and asked for his help. The staff of Donner lab were called together and requested to look into the fallout problem. Among those assembled was Dr. John Gofman, a brilliant scientist and the man who isolated the first gram of plutonium during the Manhattan Project. A medical doctor with a Ph.D. in nuclear and physical chemistry, Gofman was then hard at work on a study of heart disease. Still, he agreed to help.

"It was obvious," Gofman said later, "that the Pauling and Lewis calculations depended upon extrapolating results from high dose radiation to low dose radiation. So I said to John and Ernest that neither Pauling nor Lewis could *prove* that the extrapolation was valid, though it *might* be valid."

Ernest Lawrence was greatly relieved. Here he had a noted scientist, equal in stature to Pauling, who could testify that the chemist had no certifiable proof of his extraordinary allegation. In fact, Lawrence even persuaded Gofman to accompany him to a meeting of the California Board of Regents to make the point.

The countercampaign was underway. John Lawrence told a hushed audience at Oregon's Reed College that the effects of radiation from testing fallout were about "three percent more than the natural radiation we get." He reminded his listeners that mankind was "continually receiving radiation from cosmic rays coming down from outer space and from the natural radioactivity in the earth's crust and in the buildings in which we live and in everything surrounding us."

Gofman continued the argument in a speech before the Public Relations Society of America in San Francisco. "There exists no valid evidence," he asserted, "that any harmful effects will accrue to men individually or to their descendants. I did not say there will be no such effects," he added in an aside, "but rather that no acceptable evidence now exists that there will be." Both speeches were reported by the United Press under bold headlines like "SCIENTISTS DEBUNK 'SCARE STORIES' SENT OUT ALL OVER THE WORLD."

The Plumbbob series was supposed to begin on May 15, 1957. But the weather was uncooperative and the first blast was delayed two weeks. In the meantime, life in Las Vegas went on unfettered by the excitement and controversy swirling around the bomb tests.

In the seven years since the test site was first opened, Las Vegas had been transformed from a quiet Union Pacific railway stop into a city of lights and excitement. The entertainment spectacles at the city's casinos rivaled the best offerings of Broadway. Along the neon-lighted Strip, the blackjack and craps players nonchalantly ignored the activity only a few miles away. Between 1950 and 1957, this once-quiet city had doubled in size. The metropolitan population numbered nearly 102,000 according to 1957 census data compiled by the state.

Though the bomb tests of the AEC were delayed and postponed interminably, auto salesman "Boob" Jones proudly advertised in the Las Vegas *Sun* that there was "NO DELAY AT BOOB'S!" Jones proclaimed in a three-inch-high banner that at his car lot the "ATOM DROPS ON HIGH PRICES. PRICES ARE SMASHED!"

On the popular record charts, Pat Boone's "Love Letters in the Sand" edged Elvis Presley's "Teddy Bear" out of first place and stayed there four consecutive weeks. Comedian Joe E. Lewis and dancer Lili St. Cyr were the top attractions at the El Rancho Vegas. Teresa Brewer and Victor Borge were the headliners at the Sahara Hotel. Carol Channing's shows were sold out at the Tropicana and Liberace was pulling them in at the Riviera. For the hotels along the fabled Strip, it was a glittering summer. The Las Vegas casino operators and merchants were worried more about tourists being scared away by the bomb testing than fallout.

Finally, after two weeks of delays, the Plumbbob series blasted off on Tuesday, May 28, with the explosion of a 12kt bomb called "Boltzman." Most of the Plumbbob shots were named for deceased scientists, a practice that infuriated the dissidents opposing the testing. Two hundred and fifty Armed Forces personnel witnessed the Boltzman shot from News Nob, 11 miles away. The flash of light from the fireball was seen in San Diego — 350 miles away.

Boltzman's unusual "double-mushroom stalk" rose to a height of about 35,000 feet, where it was caught by northwesterly winds and drifted away. Monitoring the cloud's movement were 31 different aircraft tied in by radio to two brand-new electronic computers developed specifically to help forecast fallout patterns.

However, as usual, the fallout cloud didn't follow any predictable patterns. It veered off from its course and dumped radioactive debris on Quincy, a small California town. The fallout triggered an alarm among residents when Geiger counters began "clicking like crazy." AEC officials quickly branded the fallout as "no cause for alarm. The radiation is about the same," they explained, "as that humans are subject to from the earth itself and from cosmic rays."

Twenty miles from ground zero, AEC clerk-typist Ann Mark watched the Boltzman blast from a group of bleachers set up for the commission employees. Each of the shots had a festive atmosphere.

In the predawn hours, the clerks, accountants, secretaries, mechanics, plumbers and carpenters who worked at Camp Mercury would load aboard buses for the ride to their observation point. There, with collars turned upward against the early-morning desert chill, they would wait patiently for the explosions. Even though their jobs entailed nothing more than typing memos or fixing leaky faucets, the bomb blasts gave these nontechnical AEC employees a feeling they were part of the pioneering achievements.

Though they were never issued any radiation film badges, the observers were all given foggy-lensed goggles. From 20 miles away, the blast were nothing less than spectacular. Their terrible beauty lit up the sky with variant hues of reds, yellows and oranges.

Ann Mark thoroughly enjoyed each of the shows, until the June 24 blast of "Priscilla," a 37kt bomb detonated from a balloon. It was then that Mark began to have second thoughts about the tests. Watching the Priscilla fireball rise into the heavens, Mark could feel a wave of warm air reddening her face. For the first time, her mind drifted to thoughts about the terror such bombs must have wrought at Hiroshima and Nagasaki.

Another observer at some of the shots that June was Shepard Schwartz. A psychologist, he had traveled to Nevada to coordinate the preliminary preparations for yet another series of stress tests for HumRRO.

Schwartz's mission was twofold: the primary objective was to orient HumRRO researchers to the problems associated with training troops for participation in atomic warfare. A secondary objective was to gather data to help plan future Army training courses that would teach troops enough about atomic warfare to avoid panic.

Initially, the HumRRO team planned to participate in a test of the Army's new tactical organization, known as a "battle group," during

Exercise Hill and Dale, scheduled for August 19. Arrangements were made for the researchers to use troops of the recently formed First Battle Group from Fort Lewis, Washington, as their subjects.

The U.S. Army was in the midst of a great transition. Army Chief of Staff General Maxwell Taylor had convinced President Eisenhower that the advent of atomic weapons rendered the Army's traditional battlefield tactics obsolete. During World War II, the Army's fighting divisions consisted of a tripartite organization made up of three regiments of infantry with supporting artillery units.

"We sometimes experimented with a fourth infantry regiment in the airborne," said General "Jumpin' " Jim Gavin, commander of the 82nd Airborne Division during the war and one of the heroes of the Normandy invasion. "We liked it because it created greater all-around strength to the division. After the war," Gavin explained, "we began to consider the possibility of using tactical nuclear weapons. We felt that the combat divisions would have to be far more flexible and responsive to a battle-field that demanded greater mobility in the face of greater firepower."

That led logically to the creation of a "pentomic" division, made up of five battle groups. This system called for a wide dispersal of troops over the battlefield, thereby lessening the odds they would all be wiped out by a single, well-aimed A-bomb.

"Smoky," the shot scheduled for August 19, provided the Army tacticians with the opportunity to put their pet pentomic theory to the test with a real battle group maneuvering after the blast of an atomic bomb. It also provided HumRRO with a chance to do its own testing.

The psychologists were interested in two basic areas of research. First, they wanted to assess the extent to which soldiers' performance of a highly learned combat task might be impaired following their first ex-posure to an atomic detonation. The researchers hypothesized that the troops might be shocked, bemused or even panic-stricken when they were asked to traverse radioactive terrain. That led to the second area of inquiry. Traditionally, to a soldier in combat, the ground is a friend. But in atomic warfare, the ground might well be contaminated. The psychol-ogists wanted to know if fears of radiation would impair the soldiers' ability to perform.

As Schwartz explained it, the idea for the experiment at Shot Smoky had its genesis in the Civil War battle for Petersburg, Virginia. "The Union troops did some fancy tunneling and blew a huge hole in the

Confederate lines," Schwartz said. "But instead of capitalizing, taking advantage of the half-hour they had won by disrupting the rebel ranks and outflanking nearby Richmond, the Union troops stood and gawked at the hole they had blown and failed to act. We wanted to find out if well-trained troops would also stand and gawk at the explosion of an atomic device."

Several performance tests were devised to check the theory. They included a combat infiltration course which the soldiers would be required to traverse after the bomb blast, the usual questionnaires, and, most importantly, a rifle disassembly-reassembly test to determine if the soldiers' proficiency was impaired.

The questionnaires and even the rifle test all had been tried at previous exercises in Nevada. What was the purpose of exposing yet another group of soldiers to the atomic bomb? HumRRO historian Dr. Saul Lavisky said, "The Smoky tests were really just of a confirmatory nature . . . we were trying to find something new." While team leader Schwartz began making the necessary preparations for the arrival of the rest of his team of nine psychologists, the AEC continued exploding bombs in the Plumb-bob series. Unfortunately, because of weather problems, the tests were more off schedule than on.

Pigs again played a major role as experimental subjects at the Priscilla blast. Because of the failure of earlier uniform tests, 75 of 706 porkers were again dressed in "futuristic antiradiation" uniforms of various fabrics and materials. The burst was delayed so often, several of the swine outgrew the special uniforms made for them. In typical bureaucratic fashion the Army scientists had new uniforms made, rather than trying to find more slender pigs.

Six hundred and thirty-five other pigs also were exposed to the not-so-tender mercies of Shot Priscilla at distances from ground zero ranging between 2,630 and 9,490 feet. They were the subjects of biomedical experiments designed to tell the Army what sort of casualties might be expected at an atomic blast.

Unprotected, some of the pigs were placed in pens near ground zero. Between the pigpens and the bomb itself, glass screens were erected. By examining holes in the glass made by rocks and steel fragments thrown by the blast, the scientists hoped to be able to predict the trajectory of debris and the blast patterns of future explosions.

A remotely operated movie camera was focused on the pigpen

throughout the experiment. The camera dispassionately recorded the porkers' frightened distress as they frantically ran around the confines of the pen, trying vainly to escape the blast. When the Army technicians returned to the pen to pick up their stricken charges after the detonation, they found some of the animals clinging to life in spite of terrible, bloody wounds.

An Army training film incorporating some of the Priscilla footage depicts a pathetic scene: soldiers carrying the wounded animals to waiting trucks, the pigs' entrails dragging behind their battered bodies.

Despite the casualties in the pigpen, a report of the experiment written by technicians at the Walter Reed Army Hospital in Washington, D.C., listed ionizing radiation as "the decisive injurious agent in nearly all casualties." The AEC lauded the uniformed pigs' sacrifice as an important "contribution to the design and composition of military uniforms."

President Eisenhower told a press conference after the third blast of the series that he favored a complete ban on atomic weapons tests as proposed by the Russians. But Ike qualified his statement, saying that a ban was only acceptable under an inspection-protected agreement outlawing for all time the use of nuclear weapons in war.

Eisenhower pointedly explained that it would be foolish for the U.S. to lag behind any other nation in atomic weapons as long as there was a chance of their being used in war. Testing, the President emphasized, was the only way of assuring that we did not fall behind. Privately Ike expressed grave doubts to close aides and friends about the wisdom of the United States' massive production of atomic weapons.

The Soviets were winning a propaganda war of great importance. Kremlin leaders were loudly calling for a ban on the testing and pointing to the United States' insistence on continuing the blasts in Nevada as evidence that Americans were warmongers, anxious for imperialistic conquests. The Russians were winning converts among developing nations throughout the world while neglecting to mention that they themselves could be the first to declare a unilateral test ban, but refused to do so.

At his June press conference, Eisenhower took the opportunity to take a swipe at the American scientists demanding an end to the testing. He said the opposition "looks almost like an organized thing," implying that perhaps the Soviets were behind the protests. Ike also derided the leaders of the test ban movement, arguing that some of the most vocal critics seemed to be out of their own fields of competence.

While Eisenhower was attacking the credibility of the nuclear critics, AEC commissioner Dr. Willard Libby was on Capitol Hill, downplaying the risks of the nuclear tests before the Joint House-Senate Atomic Radiation Subcommittee.

"Testing constitutes a small risk — very small compared to ordinary risks which can be tolerated," Libby confidently testified in the face of overwhelming evidence that he was wrong. "Are we willing to take this very small and rigidly controlled risk?" he asked rhetorically, "or would we prefer to run the risk of annihilation which might result if we surrendered the weapons which are so essential to our freedom and our actual survival?"

The campaign for a nuclear test ban kept mushrooming, though. Two powerful Democratic senators, Mike Mansfield of Montana and Arkansas' J. William Fulbright, added their voices to the chorus urging Ike to accept the Russians' proposal for a test ban, provided that the inspection guarantees were adequate. A crusade to send the leaders of the world's nuclear powers copies of photographs of 10,000 babies was launched at a Methodist church conference in Redlands, California. The blasts in Nevada still continued.

On Friday, July 5, the largest A-bomb ever set off in the continental United States was detonated from a balloon-suspended platform 1,500 feet above the parched ground of Yucca Flat. The cloud from the 74kt Shot Hood rose 49,000 feet into the air, more than four times the height of its namesake mountain.

Two thousand Marines huddled in trenches five and a half feet deep only three and a half miles from the bomb. The dust was so thick that 34 helicopters scheduled to carry the leathernecks toward ground zero were temporarily grounded. Fifteen minutes after the blast, the helicopters lifted off with Marines aboard and touched down near the detonation point where defensive "perimeters" were formed.

The explosion woke up Las Vegas and the flash was seen as far north as Canada and 800 miles west, where the pilot of an airliner flying toward California from Hawaii saw the man-made sun light up the sky. At Groom Mine, 35 miles north of the test site, Hood shattered windows, blew open doors and bulged metal buildings. According to a newspaper report, AEC officials were searching for mine owner Dan Sheahan so an adjuster could make an inspection of the damage.

Ten days later, Shot Diablo, a 17kt bomb, was detonated. Diablo was a reluctant A-bomb. It had been scheduled to explode on June 28, but it misfired. When the device finally worked, the blast was true to its name, bathing the sky with an unusual purple, blue and lavender flare.

Two thousand yards from ground zero, a group of volunteers from the Naval Radiological Defense Laboratory and the AEC sat through the explosion in a prototype steel bomb shelter buried under a three-foot mound of dirt. They emerged several hours later, apparently unscathed. But the shelter itself was another story. The AEC had planned to bulldoze the dirt away from the shelter so the entire structure could be dug up and analyzed, but radiation levels were so heavy the shelter retrieval was delayed for several days.

At Salt Lake City, the radiation levels in the air over the city reached their highest point after the Diablo shot. Monitors measured the activity to be ten times greater than any previous record. As usual, the AEC assured residents that even the higher levels of radiation were "no cause for alarm."

In Carson City, Nevada, the atomic savants told a group of health experts that most reports of the Nevada test fallout were "exaggerated." Nevada was chosen as the site of the tests, they explained, because of its "sparse population." The government nuclear experts also admonished the group not to subscribe to the antitest fervor. "Remember," one scientist ominously warned, "if the Russians get the advantage, it could mean the end of this nation as we know it."

The public distrust of the weapons testing program also presented a vexing problem for the Air Force, which was then planning to introduce new air-to-air nuclear-tipped missiles into its arsenal. Nearly a year before the Plumbbob series, the Air Force generals asked for, and received, permission to conduct a live test of their new MB-1 *Genie* missile in the summer of 1957. *Genie* was designed to intercept an entire formation of enemy bombers at an altitude of 18,000 feet and neutralize them by exploding in their midst.

The Continental Air Defense Command (CONAD) was preparing to deploy the missiles throughout the nation. If an enemy attacked the United States, part of the battle would certainly be fought in the air, above major population centers. Americans had not experienced war within their borders since Appomattox, and the Air Force brass knew that long before any future battles would be fought, a public relations skirmish over acceptance of the *Genie* would first have to be won.

CONAD's commander, General Earl Partridge, dumped the delicate assignment in the lap of his public affairs officer, Colonel Barney Oldfield, and told him it was his job to convince the American public that it was safe, and necessary, to have nuclear missiles practically in their backyards.

About this time, five officers walked into Oldfield's office and volunteered to stand under the blast of the *Genie* firing at Shot John, scheduled for July 19. They were the answer to the public relations man's prayer.

Among them, the five officers had 22 years of experience and training in atomic weaponry. Besides that, they were all confident that the missile would do what it was intended to do and anxious to show the public that a nuclear battle could take place at 18,000 feet without harming people on the ground.

At the Baghdad Hotel in downtown Las Vegas the morning of the test, Oldfield hit on yet another gimmick to make the feat of the five officers more memorable. He took the cardboard insert out of a shirt that had just been returned from the hotel laundry, dipped his finger into a bottle of ink and wrote "GROUND ZERO — POPULATION 5" across it in broad, black letters. He then gave the sign to the sixth, unheralded volunteer of the mission, Air Force photographer George Yoshitake, who was to record the event for posterity.

The five officers, Colonel Sidney Bruce, Lieutenant Colonel Frank Ball and Majors Norman Bodinger, John Hughes and Don Luttrell, were trucked to Yucca Flat along with Yoshitake to wait for the blast. At precisely 7:00 A.M., the *Genie*, with its relatively small 2kt nuclear warhead, was triggered from an Air Force F–89 Scorpion flying at 20,000 feet. The pilot of the jet, Captain Eric Hutchinson, pulled sharply back on his stick to maneuver the aircraft into a "back flip" to escape the blast. Three seconds later, the missile exploded right over the heads of the six men at ground zero.

Major Bodinger, wired with a microphone, did a running commentary on the test, describing the blast, its flash and the heat wave that bathed the volunteers far below. "The colors are brilliant," he said excitedly, "swirling and changing . . . and now we're getting the shock waves." The concussion of the shock wave temporarily interrupted the commentary. When Bodinger's microphone returned to life, listeners could hear the jubilant shouts of the officers.

The five volunteers, led by "Mayor of Ground Zero" Sid Bruce, embarked on a triumphant nationwide tour, spreading their message: "We may never need to use the *Genie* or similar warheads, but if it happens, look at us. All of us survived in good shape."

They served as living testimonials to the effectiveness and safety of using the defensive weapons. At the same time, they helped the Air Force win wide acceptance for stationing the missiles across the land. Dr. Edward Teller and the joint chiefs of staff hailed the officers' act as one of unprecedented heroism. To Oldfield, it was simply "one of the greatest public reassurers of all time."

In the midst of all this, troops of the First Battle Group from Fort Lewis began arriving in Nevada on July 20. All of the soldiers were from units of the 12th Infantry and under the command of Lieutenant Colonel Frank W. Keating. Assigned to be part of Task Force Warrior, the soldiers were supposed to maneuver after the August 19 explosion of Smoky. But the test series was behind schedule, and Keating was told that seven other bombs had to be exploded before Smoky.

The 600 men of the First Battle Group spent the next month swept up in a cloud of heat, dust and ennui. They billeted in a primitive tent city near Camp Desert Rock, practicing combat maneuvers of the flatlands by day and playing cards to while away the evening hours. Among them was Donald Coe, a 24-year-old private first class from the town of Tompkinsville, Kentucky.

Coe remembers the dirt-floored, 11-man squad tents well. Conditions were less than luxurious. Latrines were nothing but open trenches, and the showers consisted of portable water bags held aloft on poles. Some of the soldiers got passes to travel into Las Vegas aboard buses, but Coe "didn't want to go. I just sat on the bunk and played cards. I was doing all right for a while too. We got doubles for blackjack and a quarter for twenty."

A 225-pound six-footer, Coe was more interested in trying to add to his meager private's pay in informal blackjack games than risking what few dollars he had on the professional gambling tables in the city.

Back at Camp Desert Rock, Colonel Keating was hard at work with other Army commanders writing the scenario for the Smoky exercise. Their battle plan called for troops to dig protective trenches five and a half to six feet deep within four hours using only the equipment they normally would have in the field. Then the task force was to be moved by helicopter after the blast to an objective area where the soldiers would attack "enemy" positions and capture them. The last part of the three-pronged exercise developed by Keating and the others was the resupply of the task force by air and, finally, the evacuation of the troops.

Most of Task Force Warrior was made up of the 12th Infantry soldiers. But there were others. Attached to the task force were two helicopter battalions from Fort Benning, Georgia, an elite Pathfinder team drawn from the ranks of the 82nd Airborne Division, and a platoon of the Queen's Own Rifles from Calgary, Canada. Unlike the 12th Infantry soldiers, these others were comfortably ensconced at comparatively "plush" Camp Desert Rock.

The training for Donald Coe and his fellow infantrymen was pure boredom. Day after day they maneuvered across the desert under the hot sun, attacking objectives and heaving dummy grenades at imaginary foes. They also received a full 12 hours of instruction on the proper way to board and debark helicopters. The only relief from the routine came when they were trucked to Yucca Flat to serve as observers at some of the shots. According to Coe's official Army records, prior to Shot Smoky, he was present at Shot Kepler, a 10kt device exploded on July 24; Shot Owens, a 9.7kt device on July 25; Shot Stokes, a 19kt device on August 23; and Franklin Prime, a 4.7kt device exploded on August 30.

When the First Battle Group soldiers attended their first atomic blast on July 24, the event sent HumRRO team leader Shep Schwartz reeling. After all, the main objective of the research plan he had devised was to test the performance of soldiers on the occasion of their first exposure to an atomic bomb. But Donald Coe and others lost their "atomic innocence" when they witnessed the explosion of Shot Kepler. They no longer were useful subjects for the psychological tests since their reactions would certainly be colored by their previous experiences.

But all was not lost. On July 31, Schwartz learned that another group of soldiers was due to arrive at Camp Desert Rock on August 12 to watch the Smoky blast. They were a group of paratroopers, a provisional company made up from the ranks of the 82nd Airborne Division and designated in Army reports as "Task Force Big Bang." Schwartz immediately sent a request to the Continental Army Command asking that the Big Bang troopers be assigned to HumRRO for psychological testing. Approval was granted on August 5, and Schwartz was back in business.

Late in the afternoon of August 12, the Globemaster carrying Russell Dann and his fellow paratroopers touched down at Indian Springs Air Force Base. The troopers ate dinner at the base mess hall and then boarded buses for the last leg of their journey to Camp Desert Rock.

Camp Desert Rock was a bustling Army village in 1957, lying in a broad, arid valley 65 miles northwest of Las Vegas on a spur three miles from U.S. 95. At an elevation of 3,200 feet, the camp was surrounded by mountains. The highest ground was the Specter Range, distant to the south and west. Beyond the jutting peaks, the Colorado River meanders toward Hoover Dam and Lake Mead. Closer to the north and east, toward the test site at Yucca Flat, Skull Mountain and the Spotted Range loomed above the camp.

In the seven years since the isolated tent community was established for Operation Ranger, the post had grown into an impressive installation. There were about 150 permanent buildings, an airstrip, motor pool, library, medical center, post office, volleyball court, two softball fields, an officer's club and a noncommissioned officer's club. There was also a beer hall for the lower ranks, a barber shop, dry cleaning and laundry concessions, and a general store. These facilities, housed in Quonset huts and prefabricated buildings around the camp, rang up more than $140,000 in business throughout the summer of 1957. When the 82nd Airborne troopers arrived, Camp Desert Rock was at its peak population of more than 5,000.

The 23-mile ride from Indian Springs to Camp Desert Rock took the better part of an hour. U.S. 95, a two-lane, black-topped highway, was treacherous in the waning daylight hours. More than one bus had skidded off the road at a winding curve, earning the highway its macabre nickname, the "widowmaker."

It was dark by the time the troopers arrived at Camp Desert Rock. The men shivered as they piled out of their bus into the brisk night air. The soldiers were led to a supply building just south of the beer hall where cots, mattresses, blankets and linens were stored.

Pairing off with the company bugler, Specialist Fifth Class Faith

Douglas, Dann grabbed the end of two cots and the men carried them back to their assigned Quonset hut. Then Dann and Douglas returned to the supply building to pick up their mattresses and bedclothes.

Captain Stovall placed Staff Sergeant Paul Cooper in charge of Dann's Quonset hut, since he was the senior NCO. But Cooper didn't have to issue any orders. The 20 men assigned to the hut all pitched in to assemble the cots in double tiers. They were anxious to get their living quarters squared away. It had been a long, tiring flight from Fort Bragg and most of the men wanted to get some sleep.

Dann set his field gear on the narrow shelf behind his bunk, searched in vain for a couple of hangers for his "Class A's" and, failing to find any, packed the uniforms back into his duffel bag and crawled under his blanket. Douglas clambered up onto the bunk above him just in time to hear the sounds of taps waft from loudspeakers as Cooper called for "lights out." It was 10:00 P.M., and Dann had no trouble drifting off to sleep.

5

THE GUINEA PIGS OF
CAMP DESERT ROCK

"Roll out of that rack, Douglas." The gruff voice of the company first sergeant interrupted Dann's dreams as the old-timer rousted the bugler out of the bunk above him. Dann sat up on his own bed, stretched his arms and yawned, trying to shake the last vestiges of sleep from his head while Douglas jumped down from his bunk.

"Captain wants you to blow reveille at zero-five-thirty. We're going out for P.T." The sergeant turned and crossed the room to the rack where Paul Cooper was sleeping soundly.

"Time to rise and shine, Paul," he said. "We're heading out for P.T. before breakfast. Tell your men that the uniform is gym shorts, boots, pistol belt, suspenders, bayonet and rifle."

"O.K., Top," Cooper replied as he bounded form his bed, apparently awake instantly. "I'll roust 'em."

Dann glanced at his watch. It was 5:15 A.M., and the morning sun had not yet begun to slice through the pitch-darkness enveloping the camp. He slipped his gym shorts over his skivvies, grabbed a towel and headed out the Quonset door. The young corporal made a beeline for the latrine, determined to beat the rush to the building that was certain to follow the first peals of reveille. As he filled one of the wash basins with warm water, he could hear the sharp strains of Douglas' bugle piercing the cool desert air.

Even before the first sergeant blew his whistle to call the paratroopers to formation, Dann was standing alongside his Quonset hut, ready for the morning's physical training. He was used to the daily exercises and actually found himself looking forward to the three-mile run that accompanied the Army's traditional "Daily Dozen" sit-ups, push-ups, squat thrusts and jumping jacks. The physical routine had left him in the best shape of his life.

"Corporal Dann!" Captain Stovall was waving to him from across the rock-strewn expanse that separated the rows of Quonset huts. The company commander was standing with a group of other officers and the first sergeant. Dann heaved his rifle to the port arms position across his torso and ran to where the officers were gathered.

"Corporal Dann reporting, sir!" Dann barked as he reached the assembled officers. Snapping to attention, Dann set his rifle butt next to the toe of his right foot in the order arms position and stiffly saluted the captain, reaching across his body with his left hand, fingers extended to the muzzle of his M–1.

"At ease, corporal!" Stovall said, casually returning the salute. "Top here tells me you doubled as P.T. cadre in your training company back at Bragg. Is that so?"

"Yes, sir, I sure did." Dann replied.

"Think you could call cadence for our P.T. while we're out here?" Stovall asked.

"Yes, sir. It'd be an honor."

"Good. We'll be moving out in five minutes. Sergeant, call the company to formation."

The first sergeant stepped away from the group and blew a shrill blast on his whistle. That quickly brought paratroopers thundering through the doors of the Quonset huts, scrambling to buckle their pistol belts as they ran. The men assembled into platoons and marched to the road adjacent to the camp buildings. After the first sergeant ordered port arms and then called for a double-time run, Dann's voice boomed out the cadence.

The chorus of 160-some voices responding to Dann's call shattered the morning calm of the camp. The paratroopers circled the camp at a dead run, singing and chanting all the way. At the portals of dozens of Quonset huts, other soldiers appeared to see what all the fuss was about. Rubbing the sleep from their eyes, they stared incredulously at the jogging, shouting paratroopers.

The blowing of reveille by the company bugler and the morning runs and exercises were all unique to the paratroopers. The rest of the camp was awakened by the skipping sound of a scratched record playing reveille over a loudspeaker, and as for the exercises, none of the other soldiers even bothered.

The predawn activity of the 82nd Airborne Provisional Company was Captain Stovall's idea. He wanted to set his troopers apart from the other soldiers. It wasn't long before he was ordered to *keep* them apart. Within a couple of days after arriving at Camp Desert Rock, Stovall was told in no uncertain terms by the camp commander that the morning runs were to take place outside of Desert Rock proper. The ruckus was disturbing the rest of the camp.

After running around the entire camp area three or four times and covering about three miles, the paratroopers spread out in a field and began to go through the Daily Dozen. In all, the physical training took about half an hour. Then it was back to the Quonset huts where the men changed into their fatigues and headed to the chow hall for breakfast.

The mess halls were the largest structures in all of Camp Desert Rock. Centrally located, they towered above the rest of the buildings, as they were elevated on concrete footings four steps above the desert floor. The other Quonset huts and permanent structures of the camp were on concrete slabs at ground level. The food was typical Army fare — palatable, but certainly not a gourmet's delight. Whatever the meals lacked in flavor was usually made up for by the fact that the soldiers' activity kept them hungry and ready to eat any offering.

The first two days in Nevada were uneventful for the paratroopers. Besides the morning exercises, they had no other duties. The soldiers passed the time, straightening out their living quarters and searching for simple amenities, like hangers, which would make their stay at Camp Desert Rock a bit easier. They were free to roam the camp, seeing what it had to offer. Inevitably, most of them ended up at the NCO and EM clubs where they guzzled beer, talked tough and regaled each other with tall tales of past exploits.

Coincident with the arrival of Task Force Big Bang, members of the HumRRO team began drifting into camp in twos and threes. The psychologists had been recruited for the mission from across the nation. Some were HumRRO veterans of other Nevada operations; the rest traveled west solely for the 1957 test.

Dr. Boyd Mathers, a graduate of the University of Minnesota, joined HumRRO in 1953. Though he wasn't really involved in the drafting of the 1957 study plan, Mathers had been asked to take a leave from his position at HumRRO's Fort Knox Armor Division to help out with the tests' administration.

Dr. Ralph Kolstoe, a four-year HumRRO veteran, agreed to travel to Nevada from Washington, D.C., to join the effort. He was promised that the exercise would be over by Labor Day. That would give him an opportunity to return to Washington in time to pack up his family and drive to North Dakota, where he had already accepted a position on the state university faculty.

Most of the others also were asked to join the team on a temporary basis. Dr. Bob Baldwin came from HumRRO's D.C.-based Training Methods Division along with William Montague and Dr. Robert Vineberg. From the Leadership Human Research Unit came Christian Peterson. The HumRRO Infantry Human Research Unit at Fort Benning, Georgia, sent Howard Sarvis and Robert Schroeder. Traveling to Nevada with Mathers from Fort Knox was John Cook. Including Shep Schwartz, the HumRRO team numbered ten psychological experts.

Nine paratroopers from the 82nd also were drafted for the team. They served as assistant monitors, helping the psychologists with record-keeping, timing the troops' actions and taking care of administrative details.

The HumRRO team was housed at Camp Desert Rock. But they lived in more well-appointed luxury than the enlisted soldiers. Like the officers' barracks, the wooden hut housing the psychologists was equipped with a pair of "swamp coolers." These were primitive air conditioners that operated on a humidifying, evaporative principle. Water was pumped over thick cellulose pads. A fan aimed against the pad blew cool, moist air into the hut. The process kept the building surprisingly comfortable in the hot, dry desert.

Some of the researchers wore Army fatigue uniforms with a patch saying, "Scientific Observer" on the sleeve to distinguish them from the soldiers. The rest were garbed in a variety of clothes. Work clothes, shorts, tennis clothes or almost anything else that provided protection against the elements was acceptable. Nearly all of the psychologists wore baseball caps as a hedge against sunstroke.

It didn't take long for the novice team members to learn what old-time "desert rats" already knew. Temperatures in the desert fluctuate more than those of more humid areas. The clear air subjects people to brilliant sunshine during the day and severe cold at night when unsheltered warm objects, including people, give up their heat rapidly. The only way to live comfortably with the desert is to always wear long-sleeved shirts, full-length trousers and a broad-brimmed hat. Sturdy, comfortable shoes are a must as protection against the sand, rocks, scorpions and rattlesnakes.

Two days after the paratroopers arrived at Camp Desert Rock, they were assembled in the post theater for a lecture by the HumRRO team. Waiting for the soldiers was a bedraggled group of scientists who droned on about their mission and explained in terms a bit more specific than most of the soldiers could understand the purpose of the soldiers' presence.

Before beginning their lecture, the scientists presented a film of the Bikini bomb blasts. When the lights went out, so did many of the paratroopers. Taking advantage of the darkness, dozens of men drifted off to sleep and had to be awakened for the HumRRO presentation.

The researchers explained that they intended to test the paratroopers' skills before and after Smoky by timing their performance on an infiltration course and during rifle disassembly and reassembly tests. After the lecture, the monitors passed out questionnaires for the soldiers to complete.

The first few questions on the form were innocuous enough. They asked for basic information on the soldiers' educational background, rank and Army experience. These were followed by a series of questions designed to gauge the troopers' attitudes and knowledge about atomic bombs. The bulk of the questionnaire was made up of interrogatives concerning the effects of atomic bombs. Many of the questions only served to increase the troopers' anxiety about what awaited them on Yucca Flat.

According to the HumRRO analysis of the questionnaire responses, 39 percent of the men "incorrectly" thought that "radiation from an A-bomb explosion would make men in foxholes 1-1/2 miles away permanently sterile." Thirteen percent "correctly" guessed that it would be safe to walk through ground zero "immediately after" an A-bomb was exploded 2,000 feet above the ground. Only 6 percent "correctly" thought it would be safe to drink water in open tanks a mile away from an A-bomb immediately after the bomb was detonated.

The psychologists culled the questions, along with the "correct" answers, from Army field manuals on atomic warfare. Apparently, however, few of the soldiers from the 82nd had ever read the manuals — or believed them. Instead, they were suspicious and skeptical. They glossed over their worries with humor and, like good soldiers, were all prepared to follow orders to the letter, regardless of their feelings.

The HumRRO researchers asked if the soldiers had any questions for them. "They were all kind of dumb questions," recalled psychologist Boyd Mathers. "Somebody asked what the possibility was of becoming sterile while participating in the exercise. He was told, well, if you hold your balls up on a stick, that would probably do it."

After the lecture, the paratroopers marched to an open stretch of desert adjacent to Camp Desert Rock, where a practice infiltration course had previously been prepared by post engineers. Smoky was scheduled to go off five days later, so intensive training in preparation for the blast had to begin.

The course was 80 yards long and 20 yards wide. Standing four abreast, the soldiers were required to walk 10 yards from a piece of engineer's tape marking the beginning of the course to a barbed-wire barricade. The bottom strand of the barricade was only a few inches above the ground.

Each man would slide under the wire and, cradling his rifle in his arms, crawl 15 yards on elbows and knees to another wire barricade. Passing beneath that, the soldiers crawled 15 more yards to a third barricade. After negotiating the third wire fence, it was a 15-yard slither to a second piece of engineer's tape.

The second piece of engineer's tape marked the point where the troopers could get up off their knees. From there, they were asked to run 15 yards to a simulated wall constructed of baling wire suspended on pickets. At the wall were piles of dummy grenades. Fifteen yards beyond was a pit four feet wide and four feet long. The troopers were expected to drop back to the ground when they reached the wall, ready a dummy grenade, rise up and lob it into the pit. After that, the soldiers were told to crawl to the side of the course and present their weapons for inspection.

Not surprisingly, the repetitive training on the infiltration course got old rather quickly. The stretch of desert was covered with sharp-edged rocks that scuffed the troopers' spit-shined boots and tore gaping holes in their fatigue uniforms.

The HumRRO researchers, to their credit, soon surmised that the rash of torn uniforms and skinned elbows and knees wasn't doing much to help morale. The next weekend, the HumRRO team went to Yucca Flat to watch the detonation of Shot Shasta and learned that Smoky would be delayed for at least ten days. The postponement gave them an opportunity to redesign their infiltration course.

By Monday, August 19, "the crawling distance was reduced from 45 to 15 yards," reported the HumRRO researchers, "to alleviate damage to bodies and uniforms." A foxhole was dug between the second and third wire fences and the troops were instructed to sprint from the second barrier to the foxhole, remain in the hole for approximately 10 seconds and then sprint to the third barrier. Beyond that was a simulated minefield. Drawing their bayonets, the soldiers were told to drop to one knee and probe for the 12-inch-diameter tank mines with the knives.

After successfully passing through the minefield, the soldiers were in position to heave the dummy grenades. On the revised course, the required distance of the toss was reduced from 15 to 12 yards. Experience showed that fewer than half the soldiers were able to hit their targets at the longer distance.

Back at the starting tape, the soldiers spread ponchos out on the ground. On a whistle signal from the HumRRO scientists, the troops were told to field-strip their M–1 rifles, as quickly as possible while monitors timed them with stopwatches and recorded their scores. At the sound of a second whistle blast, the rifles were reassembled.

After three days of crawling on the infiltration course, the men were glad to be relieved from the drudgery for a weekend. Saturday morning was "commander's time" at Camp Desert Rock for the 82nd. The early hours were filled with an inspection by Captain Stovall, care and cleaning of weapons and barracks, and, then, the usual physical training regimen. The soldiers were off duty in the afternoon.

Dann, Newsome and Hamberger were whiling away the afternoon hours when they got their first taste of the tight security in effect on the base. The three soldiers decided to break the monotony of camp life by scaling nearby Skull Mountain. But when they headed for the gate, the military police on duty wouldn't let them pass. The trio asked permission to stroll up the road to Camp Mercury, but were told that Mercury was off limits.

The dejected troopers returned to their barracks and groused about the restricted atmosphere at the camp. Later that afternoon, the soldiers learned that they were invited to a special free show in Las Vegas. After dinner, most of the men loaded Air Force buses for the 65-mile ride to the city.

In town, bleachers were set up at the Las Vegas racetrack in front of a makeshift stage spanning the track. For an hour and a half, the soldiers were treated to the best entertainment Las Vegas had to offer. A comedian, serving as master of ceremonies, opened the show by calling for all electric lights in the park to be turned off.

When the racetrack was bathed in darkness, he asked everyone who had lighters or matches to ignite them on the count of three. The bleachers flickered into brightness. "It looks like you 'atomic soldiers' are glowing tonight," the comedian said as the band struck up a tune and the entertainers rushed onstage.

Singers Joni James, Gogi Grant and Gisele McKenzie kicked off the show with a medley of hit tunes. There were production numbers by a bevy of scantily clad showgirls interspersed with comic acts and a special rendition of "Music Music Music" by Teresa Brewer.

The soldiers were an enthusiastic audience, whooping and hollering for encores long after the show ended. But the troops were not allowed to venture into the city. Smoky was still scheduled for the following Monday, and the psychologists didn't want to lose their subjects to the charms of the Strip.

They were back at Camp Desert Rock just in time for lights out and to hear the news that Smoky was postponed. The next morning, Sunday, was church routine. After interfaith services, there was little to do but read the local newspapers and play cards. The service clubs were all closed.

On Monday, the troops attended an indoctrination lecture on atomic effects at a nearby Quonset hut that had been converted into a classroom. The steel folding chairs were uncomfortable, but a few of the soldiers still managed to drift off to sleep. The most memorable detail of the nondescript classroom was a large sign hanging above the blackboard at the front of the hut. It read: "Anything you hear here while you are here, leave here when you leave here."

The indoctrination, which had been carefully coordinated by the HumRRO team so material in their questionnaire would be covered, began with a film. Dann remembers the film opening with a scene on a street corner. One old codger, sitting under a nearby awning, turned to another and said, "This weather is all screwed up on account of those damn bombs." "Then the narrator would come on," said Dann, "and tell how foolish those people were. They don't understand what the bomb is, the narrator would say, and that there should be no fear at all."

The film was followed by a two-hour lecture on the bomb. The men were told what to expect and briefed on the nature of radiation. The lecture closely paralleled the AEC propaganda pamphlet "Atomic Tests in Nevada" and a handout given to visitors entitled "Continental Atomic Tests: Background Information for Observers."

The lecturer, a Virginian with a lilting southern drawl, was careful to include all the material contained in the HumRRO questionnaire in his presentation. The HumRRO researchers were anxious to see if the indoctrination had any effect on the soldiers' responses to their questionnaires.

"A nuclear explosion releases tremendous energy in heat, light, blast and nuclear radiation," the lecturer began. "The heat energy produces very hot gases at high pressure, and the outward movement of these gases creates a shock wave."

Drawing some wavy lines and dots on the blackboard with a piece of chalk, the Virginian explained that "nuclear radiation is released as particles and waves of energy. These waves are called gamma rays and are very similar to the sort of radiation you'd get if you had an X-ray. The particles are called neutrons and are made up of what is known as alpha and beta rays.

"Now, some of the radiation is released as soon as the bomb explodes. Most of it in fact. The rest is given off over a period of time by the 'fission products' created during the detonation. For each 20 kilotons of explosive energy, about two pounds of radioactive fission products are produced. In these two pounds are a variety of different radioactive substances varying in half-life from a fraction of a second to many years. The half-life of any substance is the period in which the radioactivity decreases or decays to one-half of its original value. In the next similar period, the remainder decays by one-half again and so on until the radioactivity mostly disappears.

"All of this doesn't really take very long. Every time the age of the radioactive material increases by seven times the radiation itself decreases by ten times. In other words, an hour after the bomb goes off," the lecturer explained, "the radiation level is only 5 percent of what it was five minutes after the burst. After seven hours, it's only one-tenth as hot as it was after an hour.

"The first thing you'll see when this bomb goes off is an intense light. Six miles away, the flash will be 100 times as bright as the sun. The blast itself will vaporize the material the bomb is made of and the firing platform or tower will become part of the fireball. As the fireball cools, the mushroom cloud you've heard or read about starts forming. This happens within a couple of seconds after the detonation. Within 10 seconds, the light will have subsided and the shock wave will have passed your position.

"The cloud, containing the fission products, the remnants of the firing platform and dirt and debris, rises high into the air. The heaviest particles and debris will drop right back down on the ground. Beyond about 7,000 feet, the immediate nuclear radiation is virtually harmless.

"As an observer during an atomic test, the position assigned you by the Nevada Test Organization will be one determined to be absolutely safe — even if you should be standing erect at the time the shock wave passes. This distance has also been calculated to be sufficient to protect you from the nuclear radiation. However, the flash of light might be dangerous. Exposure of the unprotected eye could result in a blind spot which might be permanent. This is why you must face away from the flash at the moment of detonation.

"No test is ever held when the weather indicates that there is any possibility of the radioactive 'stem' of the cloud settling back towards the observation area. You will be permitted to go forward into target and fallout areas, but only after monitoring teams have checked the areas and declared them safe.

"If highly radioactive fallout particles are deposited on or near the surface of your skin, like on your clothes or hair, and stay there for any long period of time, the beta radiation can cause you to lose your hair, discolor your skin or even burn you. This isn't likely to happen, but just in case, you should know about it.

"Beta burns look similar to burns from any other kind of heat, except they usually don't appear until about two weeks later and they take longer to heal. You can reduce the possibility of burns with simple decontamination measures, like bathing and changing clothes.

"Now, I want to debunk some of those horror stories I'm sure you guys have been told," the lecturer continued reassuringly. "It's true you can't see, feel, smell, taste or hear nuclear radiation. But that doesn't mean you have to fear it. Not too many of you can explain electricity I'll bet. But you've all learned to live with it and use it. It's the same with radiation.

"Mankind has been bombarded by radiation from outer space and from the ground beneath him since the beginning of time. Cosmic rays rain down from space upon each of us every second of our lives. We are also constantly exposed to radiation from uranium, radium and other elements in the earth itself. Granite rock, for example, contains radioactive radium, thorium and potassium. Our bodies also contain radioactive materials taken in with the food we eat and the water we drink. The sum total of this radiation is known as the 'background level.'

"Uncontrolled radiation, like uncontrolled fire or carelessly used electricity, can be dangerous," he explained. "You know the sun will give you a nice suntan, but if you are over-exposed, it can burn the skin and make you quite sick. Nuclear radiation does different things to people depending upon what kind it is, the amount to which a person is exposed and whether the whole body or only a part is exposed. Overexposure to any kind of radiation causes injury by damaging the tiny living cells which compose our bodies. The amount of overexposure determines the amount of damage.

"Your bodies can withstand considerably greater doses of radiation than from normal background because the effects are repaired almost as rapidly as they are produced. Over many years, an individual could receive in small doses a total amount of radiation which would be deadly if it was received to his whole body within 24 hours. A total of 25 to 50 roentgens will produce temporary blood changes if it's received in a brief period — but it will not cause illness. Radiation sickness usually occurs somewhere in the 75 to 125 roentgen range. You know you've got radiation sickness when you get nauseous and start vomiting. But you could recover from serious radiation illness at doses as high as 200 roentgens if you get the proper attention.

"The most sensitive part of your biological system to radiation is the inheritance mechanism. Every cell of your body contains a collection of tiny units called genes. Together, these genes determine all the characteristics a person is born with. The genes are passed on from parents to children at birth. Every so often one of these genes changes, or mutates. We know a number of ways to bring about these mutations. Heat can do it. So can certain chemicals and radiation. Any radiation dose, however small, can induce some mutations. In fact, every generation of living things gets some mutations from background radiation. They are called spontaneous mutations.

"But don't worry. The National Academy of Sciences has estimated that it would take as much as 30 to 80 roentgens of radiation directly on the reproductive organs to cause as many mutations in offspring as would occur spontaneously. The Academy has also reported that low doses of radiation have not been proven to shorten life expectancy. Even doses up to 100 roentgens, spread over many years, have not been shown to shorten human life.

"All of this brings us to one critical question. How much radiation is safe? We can't say for sure what is absolutely safe, but what we do know is that you can get quite a bit of radiation without any real significant risk of danger. We've set a permissible radiation dose limit for these tests at five roentgens. That corresponds with the limits that atomic energy workers live with. Each of you will be issued a radiation film badge when you enter the test site. Later, these badges will be analyzed to determine exactly how much radiation you've received and the amount will be entered into your records.

"Remember this," the lecturer concluded, "no observer has ever been injured by test activity at the Nevada Test Site, though there have been construction and traffic accidents. We're taking every possible measure to make sure we maintain this clean record."

After the indoctrination, the HumRRO psychologists handed out their questionnaires once again and asked the soldiers to fill them out. Many of the troopers had slept soundly throughout the lecture. They knew they were being propagandized, or as one soldier put it later, "the Army was just trying to blow smoke up our butts. I wondered if they actually think people are that dumb. Sure they said we'd be completely monitored at all times, but hell, nobody believed them. Nine chances out of ten the monitor was just some PFC assigned to the detail who didn't give a damn. Just a detail, just a job."

The skepticism of the soldiers showed in the questionnaire results. A majority still believed it would be unsafe to drink water in open tanks a mile away from the bomb blast. Most also still thought it unsafe to walk through ground zero immediately after the burst. However, the indoctrination was successful in one way. It convinced 83 percent of the soldiers that there was no danger of becoming sterile from the bomb blast if they were in foxholes a mile and a half away.

When the questionnaires were completed, the troopers were marched to the shortened infiltration course, where they practiced the routine over and over again. The first few times through the barbed wire, the men were in a competitive spirit. They tried to out-crawl, out-run, out-throw and out-field-strip each other. But the novelty soon wore off and the endless rehearsals became a chore.

The company officers didn't even bother to join in the repetitive training after the first week. Captain Stovall turned over command of the company to his top NCOs. While the soldiers repeated their maneuvers incessantly, the officers drank and played cards at their Camp Desert Rock club or traveled to Las Vegas for the attractions of the casinos.

On Friday, August 23, the paratroopers were taken onto the Nevada Test Site for the first time. The purpose of the visit was to familiarize the troops with the terrain and allow them to practice their infiltration and rifle-disassembly tests in the area they would actually occupy the day of Smoky.

The squads were assigned to their positions in the forwardmost troop trenches and briefed on the countdown procedure. They were also shown the protective position they were to take when the burst went off. After that, they ran through the rifle test and the infiltration course. As each platoon finished the infiltration course, they walked back to the trench area, where a field mess had been established for lunch.

Because no training or testing was scheduled that weekend, most of the soldiers of the 82nd got their first unrestricted passes the next day and headed for Las Vegas, sardonically referred to as "Lost Wages," to try their luck at the gambling tables. Others headed in the opposite direction toward Beatty, Nevada, and its chief attraction — a main street lined almost exclusively with houses of ill repute.

Dressed in their sharply creased khaki Class A uniforms, the "Three Musketeers" — Dann, Newsome and Hamberger — hopped the first available bus to Las Vegas. It had been three weeks since the last payday, and neither Dann or Newsome had much money to spend. But Hamberger, who had collected a small sum of winnings thanks to his prowess with a pair of dice, offered to bankroll the trio.

The soldiers were dropped off at a bus stop on Fremont Street next to a small city park. They walked briskly to a nearby casino, the Golden Nugget, and circled the gambling tables. None of the three had yet turned 21 years old. Technically, they could neither drink nor gamble legally. But Newsome, affecting his most ingratiating smile, sauntered up to one of the crap tables and noisily greeted the players and croupier like they were long-lost relatives.

Hamberger quickly set to work, flicking his wrist like a pro and making "hard fours" over and over again, doubling his bet and then doubling it again. After winning about forty dollars, Hamberger generously bestowed a ten-dollar bill on each of his two friends, who loudly egged him on as they drank the free liquor provided by casino cocktail waitresses to gamblers.

Newsome and Dann started shooting the dice too. All three men continued to win — for a while. Soon their luck and money started to run out as the law of averages got the best of them and unlucky sevens and elevens kept turning up on the ivories. With only a couple of dollars left among them, the trio set off for a bit of sightseeing.

Dann ducked into a five-and-dime store on Fremont and bought some toothpaste and shaving cream. The post exchange at Camp Desert Rock didn't carry the brands he liked. The soldiers visited the Golden Horseshoe, where they gaped at the million one-dollar bills in a glass case and then wandered down the famed Strip. All three weaved along the avenue. They were beginning to feel the effects of the free liquor they had quaffed at the Golden Nugget.

In front of one of the casinos an actor portraying a mannequin stood motionless and unblinking. The stunt was designed to attract attention to the gambling house's gate, and it worked. Women would kiss him passionately on the lips, trying to evoke some response. Children would tug at the mannequin's clothing. Nothing seemed to provoke him into movement. That is, until Dann, Newsome and Hamberger came along.

Puffed up with the false courage of alcohol, the trio teased the actor.

"You some kind of queer, pretty boy?" Newsome taunted.

"Yeah, you mean none of these women can get a rise out of you?" Hamberger laughed. "You *must* be some kind of fairy."

The three huddled on the curb and came up with a sure-fire plan to get some response from the motionless man. Hamberger circled the actor menacingly. Then, while Hamberger dropped to his hands and knees behind the man, Dann slipped his hand into his bag, pulled out the can of shaving cream and sprayed it in the actor's face while Newsome pushed the mannequin backward over Hamberger.

Cursing and spitting out shaving cream, the actor was splayed out on the sidewalk. A half-dozen guards rushed out of the casino as the soldiers ran off, laughing and slapping one another on the back. They ducked into another hotel and disappeared into the crowd, congratulating each other on their combined achievement.

Crossing the casino floor to the bar, the three sat at a table and pooled their remaining resources to buy some beer. A former paratrooper sitting at the bar came to their table and offered to buy them all drinks. They spent the early evening hours drinking and swapping stories until their money and the ex-paratrooper's interest was exhausted and he returned to the gaming tables.

By the time Newsome, Hamberger and Dann got back to the bus stop on Fremont Street, the last shuttle of the day to Camp Desert Rock had already departed. The three stretched out on park benches and sank into alcohol-laden slumber.

They awoke, slightly hung over, but with enough of their wits about them to marvel at the fact that no dew covered them. They caught the first bus back to camp and arrived in time for church. Dann dutifully went to the services, hoping to atone for his sins of the night before.

The following day, Monday, August 26, the company was back on the infiltration course, practicing the routine tests once again.

The days were starting a bit earlier that week. To escape the sweltering afternoon desert heat, the paratroopers were awakened at 4:00 A.M. for their morning run. By rising earlier in the morning, the training on the infiltration course usually could be completed by noon. That gave the soldiers their afternoons free to search for cool spots to beat the heat.

On Tuesday, the AEC announced that a small atomic bomb, "Franklin Prime," was scheduled for detonation the next day along with Smoky, just in case the explosion of the larger bomb had to be postponed because of unfavorable weather.

Some of the paratroopers came to Camp Desert Rock armed with carbines instead of M–1 rifles. Since only rifle-equipped troops were needed for the HumRRO tests, Captain Stovall asked whether the troops armed with carbines could watch the Franklin Prime explosion so at the very least they could have the opportunity of witnessing an atomic blast. The HumRRO psychologists agreed.

At 4:30 that afternoon, the AEC announced that Smoky was, indeed, postponed and the outlook for firing the bomb on subsequent days was not good because of predictions of adverse weather. The next morning, the HumRRO team, the monitors and the carbine-equipped troops were trucked to Yucca Flat to watch the Franklin Prime explosion.

It was before dawn, 5:30 A.M., when the bomb burst. Newsome was on his way to the showers after morning P.T. when "the whole world lit up. The hair on my neck stood up at attention and the air seemed to crackle around me. I turned and watched the mushroom cloud rise over the mountains to the north. It was a very emotional experience for me. My heart swelled with pride and tears came to my eyes as I watched the cloud billowing into the heavens."

Because of the postponement of Smoky, Test Manager James Reeves suggested to HumRRO's Shep Schwartz that he consider the feasibility of using another shot, not so dependent on weather conditions, for the psychological troop tests. A new minefield and infiltration course could easily be constructed, Reeves said, and there would be plenty of time prior to the detonation for a familiarization trip to the new site.

Schwartz tentatively agreed to test the troops at the explosion of a tower shot called "Galileo," scheduled for September 4. But the fact that Galileo was expected to be detonated at five in the morning created a new problem: the troops would need training under low-light conditions or artificial illumination would be needed. The HumRRO team agreed to a plan to dig new trenches 2,700 yards from the bomb with the infiltration course 1,500 yards from ground zero. But when the psychologists learned that weather might also affect the scheduled firing of Galileo, the plan was scrapped.

On Thursday, August 29, four of the HumRRO team members had to leave Camp Desert Rock, and Captain Stovall informed the researchers that he had to have his troopers on their way back to Fort Bragg by September 5 so they could participate in maneuvers planned for that week. The next day, when AEC officials predicted that Galileo might be postponed for as long as a week, the HumRRO scientists decided to conduct their tests during the detonation of Shot Wheeler, a balloon-suspended blast scheduled for September 1. Post engineers began round-the-clock operations under portable floodlights to complete the new trenches and infiltration course in time.

The psychologists noticed "a marked reduction in morale of the paratroopers'' because of the frequent postponements of the bomb blasts. Frankly, the troopers were sick and tired of the continual need to practice the elementary tasks they were expected to perform. "Most of us," Dann said later, "didn't care if they fired off the damn bomb in our back pockets, as long as they got it over with." Adding to the soldiers' disgust was the fact that they were denied weekend passes because of the uncertain firing schedule of Smoky.

Friday, August 30, was payday. The event was normally an occasion for rejoicing on any typical Army post. But Camp Desert Rock was different. It was isolated, and the paratroopers from the 82nd were angry and frustrated. For the first time since they had arrived in Nevada more than two weeks before, they all had plenty of money to lavish on liquor, rich food and women. But because they were restricted to camp, there was nowhere to spend their pay.

With $230 burning a hole in his pocket, including his monthly $55 "jump pay" allotment, Dann wandered across the camp to the NCO club, hoping to drown his sorrows in a few cans of Pabst Blue Ribbon beer.

"Hey, Pierre!" Dann called to a sergeant of the Canadian Army Queen's Own Rifles whom he had met at a previous outing at the club. "You stuck in this dump too?"

"I certainly am," Pierre replied. "However, I have been trying to devise a way to get off this bloody base all afternoon." Though the Canadian's name hinted at his French descent, his clipped Canadian accent seemed to Dann more like Buckingham Palace than Paris.

"Mind if I sit with you?" Dann asked.

"I was just planning on going out to the rear," said Pierre. "Come along if you'd like. I think it might be a bit cooler out there."

"Let me get a brew first. I'll meet you out there," Dann said as he turned and walked to the bar to buy a Pabst.

The young corporal was fascinated by the Canadian soldiers. They seemed to him the epitome of fierce fighting men. All of the Queen's Own were career men and volunteers for the Desert Rock mission. Though the Canadians generally kept to themselves, staying aloof from the U.S. soldiers, Pierre, a short, stocky 12-year veteran, had befriended the inquisitive Dann.

The first thing that Dann noticed about the Canadians was their distinctive uniforms. The 82nd Airborne troopers all wore fatigues with their trousers stuffed into their boots. The blouse distinguished the stump-jumpers from other infantrymen, who were derisively referred to as "straight-legs" by the paratroopers. The troopers considered themselves tougher, stronger, braver and better soldiers than the rest. Their jump wings were pinned proudly on the round, pillboxlike, visored field caps they wore. But the plastic insert that kept the field caps perfectly spherical cut into Dann's forehead, and the tight fatigue uniforms were notoriously uncomfortable in the blazing desert.

By contrast, the Canadians were garbed in loose-fitting, khaki-colored cotton uniforms. Their shirts, which looked like part of a safari uniform, were worn outside their trousers, allowing air to circulate. Over the shirts were buckled wide Sam Browne belts with their narrow leather straps angling across the soldiers' chests and over their shoulders. The Canadians' hats were similar to the paratroopers', but they weren't stiffened, and a large, red number "1" emblazoned each of the cap crowns.

Dann, taking advantage of the bargain price of 20 cents per beer, bought one for himself and one for his Canadian friend. A can in each hand, he passed through the back door of the NCO club onto the small, awning-covered dirt patio south of the building and sat down at a table with Pierre, proffering one of the beers.

The two men sat chatting and watching the striking sunset unfolding before them. The bright orange ball cast a shimmering glow over the barren desert landscape. The sky seemed to quiver in a multihued amalgam of brilliant color. Dust devils, minitornadoes borne of the abrupt fluctuations in temperature and wind, were whipping the air into a frenzy. Though both men had seen dozens of enthralling sunrises and sunsets during their stay in Nevada, the spectacle still entranced them.

After a few hours of jump stories and arm-wrestling matches to decide who would buy the next round, Dann convinced Pierre to walk over to the Enlisted Men's club to meet Newsome. The pair finished their beers and strolled to the club, only a few huts away.

Inside, the EM club was the antithesis of the staid decorum that characterized the NCO club. The place was packed from wall to wall with soldiers. On one side of the room was a group of loud boisterous paratroopers. They were laughing and taunting the straight-legs with catcalls. The infantrymen returned the calls with epithets and shouts. Several of the Queen's Own occupied a couple of tables toward the front of the club and were watching the shouting match with mild amusement.

In a back corner of the room sat a group of Gurkhas, oblivious to the Americans' antics.

Dann easily spotted Newsome in the midst of the group of troopers. He was half drunk, spoiling for a fight and the apparent leader of the chorus of name callers. An ear-splitting rendition of "The Stripper" blared from the jukebox, adding to the din.

"Chuck!" Dann shouted to Newsome as he crossed over to where his friend was sitting. "Cool down for a minute. I want ya to meet a friend of mine. This is Pierre."

"Well, it's right nice to meet ya," Newsome said, extending his hand. "Russ here's been telling me all about you Canadians."

They were in the middle of introductions when a fist fight broke out across the room. A "leg" had insisted on playing "The Stripper" over and over again on the jukebox. One of the troopers, who apparently had listened to the song enough, pulled the plug. The infantryman plugged it back in. The paratrooper decided to finish the argument by heaving the jukebox over, smashing it to the ground. In a matter of seconds, punches were being thrown.

Newsome grabbed Dann and pulled him aside.

"If them Gurkhas get into this fracas, Dann, get ready to run."

"What the hell you talking about, Chuck!" Dann asked as he tugged his sleeve free from Newsome's grip.

"Can't you see those curved knives they got hangin' from their belts?"

"You betcha, I can see them," Dann replied. "So what?"

"Well," said Newsome, "I hear tell they ain't supposed to stick those knives back in their sheaths once they draw 'em unless the blade's tasted blood. I even seen one prick his finger once till it bled before he put his blade away. Those Indians, they don't fight, they just kill."

"Whew," Dann said, glancing over at the Gurkhas, who were still blithely ignoring the growing fist fight in the middle of the room. "I'll keep my eye on them."

"Good," Newsome said. "Then let's go. And remember, Danny-boy, keep your left up." The Virginian let out a whoop and waded into the melee with Dann right behind him.

A couple of paratroopers backed up against one wall of the club and shouted, "We're going to throw every damn straight-leg out of this damned club."

The room erupted with flying fists as soldiers joined the fray. Even the

Canadians were drawn into the brawl. Beer bottles and chairs were smashed over skulls as the outnumbered paratroopers battled the infantrymen. Within a few minutes, shrill whistle blasts pierced the noisy sounds of battle as a dozen M.P.'s rushed into the club, brandishing their clubs.

Two of the M.P.'s grabbed one of the paratroopers and dragged him out the door while another announced over a bullhorn that the club was closed. The fight didn't end, it merely spilled out into the road. Some of the soldiers picked up stones and pelted the M.P.'s as they raced away in a jeep with an arrested paratrooper in tow. Rocks also were tossed against the sides of the metal Quonset huts, creating resounding booms.

Within a few minutes, Captain Stovall and Lieutenants Ginn and Crites ran over to the club to break up the fight. The captain's voice abruptly brought the brawl to an end. Stovall ordered the paratroopers back to their barracks and the soldiers quickly obeyed his command. They could tell that Stovall was in no mood for arguments.

Dann waved goodby to Pierre, and, with their arms draped over each other's shoulders, he and Newsome began walking back to their hut. The two men were elated by the fight. It had provided a catharsis for the frustration they felt after weeks of endlessly crawling in the desert dust.

The night air was cool and refreshing. Dann absent-mindedly looked toward the camp headquarters building and saw that the warning light on the flagpole was green.

"Hey, Chuck!" he said excitedly. "Look at that damn pole. The light's green."

"It sure is. Green as the grass on the lawn back home. Looks like they're going to shoot ole Smoky off tomorrow after all."

"We'd better get some sack time. It's going to be an early one tomorrow."

"I'm with you, pal," Newsome said. "Let's hit the racks."

When they reached the Quonset hut, Dann could hear Douglas quietly snoring on the bunk above his. He chuckled to himself as he lifted Douglas' bugle off the shelf and went outside and filled it with sand.

"This old bugle," Dann thought to himself as he poured sand into the instrument, "ain't going to blast me out of bed tomorrow."

Dann crawled into his bunk. The quiet convulsions of his silent laughter helped rock him to sleep.

6

FIREWORKS ON YUCCA FLAT

Around 2:00 A.M. on the day of Smoky, Corporal Dann was jarred awake when the bugler crawled down from the bunk above him to sound the reveille call.

Two hours earlier, AEC Test Manager Reeves had called HumRRO team leader Shep Schwartz to tell him that the blast, which had already been postponed ten times, was finally set for firing. To the members of the HumRRO team, the announcement was anticlimactic.

Wind conditions indicated that fallout from the bomb would most likely contaminate the Wheeler trenches and infiltration course that had just been prepared. The entire battery of psychological experiments couldn't be conducted until after the contamination subsided. By that time the paratroopers would be back at Bragg. The entire HumRRO mission seemed futile.

Schwartz and his associates decided that the members of Task Force Big Bang should witness the Smoky shot anyhow. Even if the stress tests couldn't be carried out, at least the paratroopers would have the opportunity to witness an atomic blast, and that would help them fulfill their original training mission at Camp Desert Rock: indoctrination in the effects of atomic weapons. If the crawling course in the Smoky area had cooled down enough within a few days after the blast, maybe there would be time to collect some data.

Only five of the original ten members of the HumRRO team were still in Nevada for Shot Smoky. But they supplemented their ranks with assistants from the paratroopers' provisional company. If there was any way to conduct the planned tests, they were going to do it.

As he lethargically donned his fatigues, Dann made a mental note to repair the rips and tears his uniform had suffered after endless hours of crawling under the strands of barbed wire on the infiltration course. He cursed under his breath the scientists who stood around with their clip-boards and stopwatches, timing every action of the troops.

The shadowy roadways of Camp Desert Rock were illuminated by only a few fire lights shining down from the portals of Quonset huts. Dann walked toward the latrine, only to be overtaken by Douglas, who was loping along, one boot on and the other in his hand.

"What's the rush, Doug?" Dann inquired innocently.

"Aw, some S.O.B. put sand in my bugle while I was asleep. I gotta wash it out quick. It's almost time for reveille!"

"Wonder who the hell would do a fool thing like that." Dann could barely contain himself.

"I don't know," Douglas answered with a twinge of anger in his voice, "but when I find him, I'm gonna wring his neck." The bugler tugged his other boot on and sped past Dann toward the latrine.

Within half an hour, the company top sergeant was blasting on his whistle, calling the paratroopers to formation. The men sluggishly wandered out of their Quonset huts in twos and threes. They stood in small groups, smoking cigarettes, talking and stamping their feet to get the blood flowing through their legs.

"When it came time for that shot," remembered Lieutenant Ginn, "we were missing about a third of the company, and I guess a third of the company there seemed intoxicated. There was almost a fist fight between an officer and an enlisted man in front of the company formation. I've never seen anything like it before or since. I was convinced that when we got back to Fort Bragg, the company commander was going to bring court-martial charges against about ten people. But it never happened. I guess everybody just wrote it off as a bad situation, best forgotten."

By three o'clock, the paratroopers had been issued radiation film badges. They were also given sandwiches for breakfast. Their canteen cups were filled to the brim with hot coffee, and some of the men sipped the bitter java as they filed onto the five-ton cattle trucks that had arrived to ferry them to Yucca Flat and their long-awaited appointment with Smoky.

The trucks were typical GI-issue: powerful diesel tractors pulling 40-foot-long flatbed trailers, all painted the familiar Army olive drab. Along the slatted sides of the trailers were low wooden benches. Two rows of benches in the middle of the bed bisected the trailers, allowing four sticks of soldiers to climb aboard with a minimum of difficulty.

The trucks lurched forward with a jerk, throwing a few soldiers who were standing toward the front into a tangled heap. Some of the men continued standing for a few minutes, but the storm of dust and pebbles kicked up by the tires of the trucks at the head of the long convoy soon discouraged the sightseeing attempts.

Donald Coe was aboard another truck bound for Yucca Flat that morning. It was a familiar trip that, by August 31, had become all too routine for him. Smoky would be the fifth atom bomb Coe had watched explode, but he knew this one was going to be different. At all the previous shots, Coe and the other soldiers of the First Battle Group had simply been observers. Now, after weeks of desert maneuvers, the men of Task Force Warrior were finally going to have the opportunity to conduct the helicopter-borne assault they had been training for.

It was for the Smoky shot that the Army and the AEC laid their most detailed plans. As at all previous exercises, the AEC was nominally in charge. Officially, the military was allowed to participate, providing that the Armed Forces operations did not upset AEC activities. All of the Army's plans needed one week's prior approval by the AEC scientists. Each time the shot was delayed, the Army commanders were forced to revise their exercise plans and switch the sites of radar installations, communications positions and observer trenches.

The final decision to fire a shot was made by Test Manager James Reeves after weather factors and fallout predictions were taken into consideration. But as long as the Army's maneuvers didn't interfere with the AEC's studies of the bombs' effects on structures and equipment, the soldiers were free to use any part of the test site for training exercises. Though the AEC contracted with the Reynolds Electrical and Engineering Company (REECO) to provide trained radiation monitors to protect government employees, the Army had its own monitors for the troops.

The Sixth U.S. Army sponsored an "extensive" training program and successfully graduated 417 experts from the Camp Desert Rock Radiological Monitoring School. Most of the monitors were from the Sixth Army, but a few 82nd Airborne "Pathfinders" also graduated from the school. The Pathfinders were paratroopers specially trained in infiltration techniques and radio-and-communications skills. Their mission at Smoky was to establish a secure landing zone and guide in the helicopters carrying the soldiers of the First Battle Group when radiation levels had subsided enough to permit a safe assault.

The Smoky test repeated many of the previous exercises. Its primary purpose was to "indoctrinate selected individuals in the effects of atomic weapons and to conduct certain specified troop and material tests of doctrine, tactics, techniques and equipment related to atomic weapons." Yet the Smoky test had another objective, one that ultimately took precedence: the Army was especially interested in actually demonstrating how effective battle groups and pentomic warfare tactics could be. That made public relations equally as important as indoctrination and training.

More reporters, cameramen and television crews were invited to watch the Smoky shot than any other test. Military photographers and combat artists abounded. A film crew was even dispatched to record the event for the Army's "Big Picture," a television series then enjoying wide popularity on the airwaves. And the newsmen were treated royally.

In an after-action report compiled by the Army months after the exercise, the brass hats candidly admitted that the real purpose of Smoky was "to portray to the public the Army at its best employing pentomic organization in operations under atomic warfare conditions." In their zeal to impress the press corps, the Army commanders may have carried their mission a bit too far.

When one of the Canadian soldiers was injured during the maneuver, the task force commander radioed a call for a helicopter to evacuate the "casualty." The helicopter touched down at the designated evacuation site, but, instead of carrying away the injured soldier, it was commandeered to transport members of the news media back to the AEC control point. Another copter had to be sent to pick up the Canadian. One general bitterly criticized the exercise for being "tailored in the form of a demonstration for observers and the press," rather than as a useful troop test.

The convoy carrying the soldiers of Task Forces Warrior and Big Bang rumbled past the Camp Mercury gate and northward on the Mercury Highway alongside Frenchman's Flat. Within a half-hour they had crossed Yucca Pass and the AEC control point onto Yucca Flat. The full moon illuminated the mountain ranges surrounding the flat and the soldiers could just make out the 700-foot Smoky tower, spotlighted "like a giant Christmas tree" before a group of rolling mountains that provided a natural border at the northern end of the valley.

The headlights of the trucks danced over the terrain, casting eerie shadows as they struck the multiarmed Joshua trees that bordered the highway at higher elevations. Sharply pronged yucca plants littered the landscape like an army of inanimate porcupines. Each of the dozens of bombs exploded in the valley had pulled tons of dirt into its whirling vortex and then dumped the debris back onto the flat, creating a fine deposit of powder that covered everything. The windstream generated by the passing trucks bounced tumbleweed along the road and whipped up a torrent of dust.

The convoy reached the Smoky trenches 4,500 yards south of the tower about 4:00, after an hour's travel. The troops filed out of the trucks and into the trenches, practicing the procedure they had been taught. But within a few minutes, they were ordered out of the trenches and back aboard their trucks. AEC weather prognosticators were worried that a sudden shift in the wind might dump the Smoky fallout directly on the trenches. Rather than cancel the blast at the last moment, the commanders decided to move the soldiers to safety.

The trucks carrying the First Battle Group raced west across the flat to a new group of hastily dug trenches. But the 82nd Airborne troopers were carried to a small hillside called Lookout Point on the northern ridge of the Banded Mountain range. Some of the men grew a bit apprehensive when they saw the detonating tower less than three miles northwest of their position. The soldiers realized they would be watching the blast from an unprotected position. There was nothing between them and the bomb but air.

At 4:45 A.M., the AEC scientists announced that H-hour for Smoky had been postponed from 5:00 sharp to 5:30. The paratroopers had almost an hour to kill. The HumRRO team, which had arrived at the trenches along with the troops, considered the delay a godsend. It would give them time to collect rifle test data that could be used as a baseline measurement for another test to be administered later. But their clipboards and charts were in a jeep a mile away and their subjects were spread out over the nearby hills. "The motivation to overcome these obstacles," they reported, "was extremely low."

Dann stretched out on the hillside. His body was shuddering and quivering, but he didn't know whether it was from the cold or anxiety about the bomb. Wrapping himself in his poncho, Dann closed his eyes and tried to sleep.

An Army combat artist sketched the sleeping soldier from an aerie atop the hill. Douglas told Dann later that the artist, an Army major, had been amazed that anyone would be composed enough to sleep only minutes before an atomic bomb was set to explode. "He probably didn't know," Dann explained to the bugler, "how hung over I was."

"Are ya cold Danny-boy?" Newsome asked as he and Hamberger sat down next to their friend.

"You betcha," Dann answered through chattering teeth. "I'm freezing."

"Well, don't you worry, pal. You'll warm up just as soon as them ole gamma rays start runnin' through ya." Newsome howled at his own maudlin jocularity. "Yeah, you'll be plenty warm."

"Yeah," Dann laughed nervously, "I guess I will."

A quarter-ton Army jeep roared up to the crest of the hill, an Army-Navy Ground Radio Communications (A–N/GRC–8) system mounted on the rear of the vehicle. A private hopped out of the jeep and began trying to calibrate the radio so the soldiers could listen to the countdown, but he couldn't quite find the proper frequency. All the troopers could hear was high-pitched whines and squeals emanating from the radio loudspeaker as the private fruitlessly tried to focus the radio onto the correct channel.

"Shit. That fool don't know what the hell he's doing with that 'Angry-8,' " Dann grumbled disgustedly.

"What the hell do you expect from a leg!" Newsome chimed in, craning his neck to watch the activity behind him.

"I'd better go help the S.O.B. or we'll never know when that bomb's about to go off. Goddamn Army." Dann threw his poncho off and walked up the hill to where the private was working on the radio.

"Let me help you with that, private. I'm a como chief."

"Sure, corporal. I just can't seem to find that damn channel. It's supposed to be 30,000 kilocycles."

"Well, look here," Dann explained patiently. "You've got your zero bead set wrong. Let me have your TL–29."

The private handed the corporal his wireman's pocketknife. Dann locked the screwdriver blade into place and promptly reset the radio frequency to zero. Then, watching the meter carefully, he clicked the switch to the proper channel and the voice of an AEC scientist thundered from the speakers.

"This is Dragnet," the voice from the loudspeakers crackled. "Stand by for time hack. In one minute the time will be H minus thirty minutes. H minus thirty minutes . . . thirty seconds . . . fifteen seconds . . . ten seconds . . . five, four, three, two, one, hack." Across the desolate flat a bright ball of orange fire blossomed as the AEC scientists fired a charge of high explosives to calibrate their instruments for the Smoky shot. The metallic voice from the radio began the final instructions for the soldiers.

"The shot you are about to witness this morning is Smoky. It is expected that the yield will be approximately three times nominal, forty-four kilotons. You are continued not to look directly at the fireball until after the initial intensity of the light has faded.

"Turn and face away from the direction of the shot three to five minutes before zero and shield your eyes with your arms. After the shot you will be told when to turn around and view the fireball. This will be approximately five seconds after zero. In the event of a misfire, remain in position with your eyes shielded until given instructions. That is all." The countdown continued with time checks every minute.

"Whew. Forty-four kilotons. Is that what he said?" Newsome asked.

"Yeah, that's right," Dann answered. "That's more than three times as big as the bomb they dropped on Hiroshima."

"This is what we suffered three weeks for? To get zapped like those Japanese. Hell, I'm ready to go home."

"Y'know, Chuck," Dann said, "they say it takes one of those atom bombs just to even set off an H-bomb. I'm glad they ain't blowing one of those up."

"Me too," Newsome replied. "If they were, I guess all you'd be seein' now is the dust of my boots skippin' on back to Desert Rock."

"Hell I would." Dann chuckled with a throaty laugh. "You'd be eating my dust, you betcha you would."

"This is Dragnet." The loudspeaker crackled once again. "H hour minus three minutes. Take your positions."

"I'll be damned if I'm gonna turn my back on that damn bomb," Dann remarked. "When it blows, I wanna see it coming!"

Newsome laid his rifle beside him and tucked his head between his knees, wrapping his arms across his forehead. Hamberger mirrored Newsome as he also got into position. Dann faced down the hill and sank to his right knee. Cradling the M–1 rifle in his left elbow, his right forearm protecting his eyes, Dann tucked his chin down and waited. His body trembled slightly as he girded for the blast. His stomach muscles tightened. The disembodied voice of the loudspeaker monotonously droned out the last seconds of the countdown.

At exactly 5:30 A.M., the AEC scientists 20 miles away sent an electronic signal to the bomb and Smoky lived up to its name. Though Dann, Newsome, Ginn, Hamberger and Paul Cooper shielded their eyes as they had been taught, they all recalled seeing their own bones, as if the flesh had instantaneously melted away. The flash of the fireball mercifully lasted only a few seconds. Some of the men found later that their exposed skin had been burned a bright pink as if they'd just stepped out on a sunny day after a winter's hibernation. But these men were already deeply tanned after weeks of desert maneuvers.

As the pupils in his eyes began recovering from the intense light, Dann heard the announcement that it was safe to look at the fireball. He lifted his head and watched the massive cloud of smoke and dust billow up into a dense cloud as the mushroom cap began forming.

The immense fireball seemed to be more smoke than fire, but its center glowed a hot pink, gradually shimmering a bright amber and blue. The Smoky detonating tower had been erected in a basin formed by a semi-circular ridge of hills. Dann glanced downward and saw the hill burst into flames. The Joshua trees covering it looked like stunted, gnarled crucifixes plunged into an inferno.

In the distance, Dann could hear the low, ominous roar of the shock wave rumbling toward him over the flat. It sounded like the thumping and bumping of a long line of freight cars crashing over broken rails. He heard the gravelly voice of his first sergeant bellow "Hit it!" from the hilltop and instinctively Dann flattened himself on the ground. Terra firma itself began to shake. First one shock wave, then another, and a mountainous tidal wave of dust, dirt and rock moving at a speed of 83 miles per hour tumbled the soldiers on the hillside over as if they were bowling pins.

The soldiers found themselves sprawled like rag dolls 15 to 20 feet from where they had been crouching only moments before. Dann's steel helmet was blown from his head, and as he picked himself up off the ground, he tried to spot it amidst the swirling cloud of dust that enveloped the entire area. It was a futile search. When Dann finally got back to Camp Desert Rock, the loss of the steel helmet cost him $3.20 for a replacement. The atmosphere on the hillside that morning could only be described as pandemonium.

About seven miles away from ground zero, 31-year-old AEC scientist

John Auxier and technician P.N. "Barney" Hensley watched the Smoky blast from the cab of their six-wheel-drive, two-and-a-half-ton truck. Their mission was to lead a convoy of AEC vehicles toward the atomized tower to retrieve instruments that had been left attached to a long steel cable stretching 2,000 yards south of the detonation point.

Every 250 yards or so along the cable were sophisticated neutron and gamma radiation monitoring stations. A large loop marked the end of the cable. Auxier and Hensley were supposed to hook the loop onto the bumper hitch of their truck and drag it to a low-radiation area where the instruments could be examined. They had performed the task at more than two-dozen other blasts and didn't expect the Smoky shot to present any special problems, but they were ready just in case.

The men were wearing standard RAD–SAFE clothing: white cotton coveralls taped tightly at the wrists and ankles, gloves, boots, goggles and respirators. Pinned to their chests were radiation film badges, and each of the men also had pocket electroscopes to record their doses. The special clothing was a must. At one of the Teapot shots, Auxier and Hensley's truck had become mired in the sand and they had to walk out of the ground zero area.

Auxier sat shivering in the cab of his truck, partly because of the chilly air and partly because, after all this time, the bomb blasts still excited him. As the mushroom cloud formed high above the flat, the two men removed their goggles, pulled up their respirator masks and tightened them. They waited patiently for a radio signal telling them they could start their engine. If they started the vehicle too soon, electromagnetic signals from the engine might interfere with the delicate telemetering operation that was then underway.

Auxier held two identical radiation monitoring instruments equipped with ionization chambers. All of the AEC teams carried a pair of the devices in case one failed to operate properly. Auxier flipped the on-switches of the meters and turned them both down to their lowest scale.

Four minutes after the detonation, the "go" signal came in over the radio and Hensley started the truck's engine and shifted it into gear, leading the convoy down Mercury Highway at top speed. The men knew they would have only seconds to pick up the instruments and hightail it back toward the control point before they were contaminated.

Hensley had the accelerator pressed flat against the floorboard as the truck sped past a juncture in the highway known as the "Buster-Jangle Wye" and turned up the fork of the road heading due north toward Smoky ground zero. As they passed by the "B-JY," Auxier watched the needles on his monitors quickly rising up the scale. He looked up and could see that their truck was directly beneath the boiling mushroom cloud. The air was thick with smoke and dust. Auxier was surprised to see high radiation readings on his monitor. They were still miles away from their destination.

With a hand on each instrument, he flicked the monitors to the next highest scale. Still the needles moved steadily up the meters. He went to the next scale, then the next, as the needles continued rising. When the truck was still at least four miles short of their goal, Auxier had already turned his monitors up to their highest scale — 50 roentgens per hour. That was a hefty dose to be playing around with.

Auxier reached over and tapped Hensley on the arm. There was no use in shouting, as he couldn't possibly be heard through his respirator above the din of the truck's engine. The driver glanced over as Auxier wildly motioned him to turn around. Moments after Auxier's signal, Hensley wheeled the big truck into a tight 180-degree turn across the shifting desert sand. The men beat a hasty retreat, followed closely by the rest of the convoy.

Of all the tests the two men had participated in, Smoky marked the only time they had failed to carry out their mission. As it turned out, the scientific instruments couldn't be retrieved until several days after the blast.

Apparently the high radiation levels weren't enough to interfere with the Army's plans to put on a spectacular show. Fifteen minutes after Smoky blew, a helicopter carrying the Task Force Warrior Pathfinders lifted off and headed for a landing zone within a few hundred yards of ground zero. Five minutes later, Donald Coe and the other troops of the First Battle Group moved from their trenches and marched toward waiting helicopters, a brisk 15-minute walk away.

Within an hour the Pathfinders reported that the landing zone was secure and radiologically safe. The first sortie of helicopters rose into the thick cloud of dust that still hovered over the battlefield like a pall. Because the dust limited visibility, the chopper pilots had to throttle back their machines as they flew the eight miles toward the landing zone.

Minutes later, the helicopters landed and the infantrymen jumped out, shouting and rushing toward their assigned objectives.

Several buildings had been constructed for the maneuvers, and obsolete World War II–vintage trucks, jeeps, artillery pieces and tanks were spread over the battlefield. The Army had dug more than a hundred different "enemy emplacements" stocked with small arms, mortars and mannequins so they could monitor the effect of the blast on military equipment. In some of the emplacements near the original Smoky trenches were live monkeys, provided for the test by Walter Reed Army Hospital.

Donald Coe and the other members of his unit charged through the heavily contaminated area, within yards of the 700-foot steel tower's mangled girders, twisted like pretzels by the bomb's furious heat. The infantrymen heaved their grenades into the demolished buildings and rusty tanks while combat photographers recorded the action.

Back at Lookout Point the paratroopers took a head count and reloaded onto the trucks. They rode down the hillside onto the flat. The entire valley was still covered by a hovering blanket of dust that resembled an early-morning ground fog. The soldiers were carried back to the Smoky trenches and unloaded again.

The trenches they had originally planned to occupy were caved in. If the soldiers had remained there, many undoubtedly would have been buried alive. The paratroopers started toward ground zero at a rout step, each man moving independently through the choking dust. The heat of the Smoky fireball crystallized some of the sand into silica and it crunched beneath their feet as they marched along. Everything was covered with dust. There was no plant life, no insects.

In the distance ahead the Smoky hills were still engulfed in flames. The troopers could hear the muffled whump-whump-whump of the helicopter blades slicing through the air above them, and occasionally they were able to catch a glimpse of the whirlybirds swooping through the haze.

They walked for nearly an hour, surveying the mangled cranes, tractors and Army vehicles near ground zero. When they reached a point within 170 yards of the atomized tower, Captain Stovall ordered his men to re-form and marched them back toward the trenches.

Army radiation technicians collected the men's film badges and passed a Geiger counter over them as they climbed aboard the trucks. Dann heard the instrument clicking rapidly when the technician reached him.

He was ordered to remove his field jacket and shake it out. Then the technician dusted off Dann's boots with a whiskbroom; that was the extent of the decontamination effort. The paratroopers were back at Camp Desert Rock in time for lunch. Most of them headed right for the showers and bathed with all their clothes on.

After church services the next morning, the paratroopers loaded buses and headed for Las Vegas. The soldiers were still angry about the events of the day before. They knew that most of the safety precautions that had been drummed into them for weeks before the blast were simply ignored. And all of their training on the infiltration course, the skinned knees and the ripped uniforms, seemed to be for nothing. Still, it was over. The next few days could be spent fulfilling their desires. Then it would be back to Fort Bragg. For the moment at least, the soldiers were feeling fine.

Sitting in the back of the bus with his friends, Dann began belting out the "Paratrooper's Song" to the tune of the "Battle Hymn of the Republic." Newsome and Hamberger crooned right along with him, grinning and stomping out the beat:

"There was blood upon the risers, there was brains upon the chute.
Intestines were hanging from his paratrooper boots.
They picked him up, inside his chute and poured him from his boots,
And he ain't gonna jump no more."

A dozen or so paratroopers on the bus loudly chimed in on the chorus:

"Gory, gory, what a helluva way to die.
Gory, gory, what a helluva way to die.
Gory, gory, what a helluva way to die.
And he ain't gonna jump no more."

Dann and Newsome continued leading the throng of singing voices as more and more of the troopers joined in the familiar ditty:

"He counted long and counted loud and waited for the shock.
He felt the wind, he felt the blast, he felt the awful drop.
He hit the ground, the sound was splat, his blood went spurting high.
And he ain't gonna jump no more."

As the bus turned the corner onto Fremont Street, the morbid chorus of the song startled passers-by walking peacefully along the row of casinos. Even in anything-goes Las Vegas, a screaming, singing group of paratroopers attracted attention.

The paratroopers spilled out of the bus, laughing and cursing. Dann, Newsome and Hamberger headed right for the Golden Nugget. They were known there now and felt confident they could get a drink. The trio downed a few beers and played craps for a while. As usual, Hamberger was winning consistently, but Dann and Newsome together were quickly losing more than their good-luck charm could make up. The trio split up, arranging to meet back at the Golden Nugget at midnight.

Newsome walked into the Lucky Strike Club. Providence must have called him there, because he won a pile of money. He also met a girl. She was short and dark-haired, with wide, blue green doelike eyes made up with the careful perfection of a Hollywood starlet. Since she happened to be the daughter of someone who worked for the club, the booze was on the house. Newsome wasted no time in taking advantage of the free liquor and the girl.

At the California Club, Dann also found a friend. The girl he met was a shy, reserved waitress. Lacking his friend's boisterous, good-ole-boy charm, Dann sidled up to her and asked politely whether she'd allow him to buy her dinner. She agreed, but her only break came at 11:00 P.M. Dann, flashing his toothiest and sincerest smile, said he was more than willing to wait.

Minutes before his date, an announcement came over the club's loudspeaker. All members of the 82nd Airborne Provisional Company were ordered back to Camp Desert Rock immediately. Voicing his apologies to the waitress, Dann found Hamberger and the two ran outside the club and flagged down one of the Courtesy Patrol trucks that was cruising the Strip in a search for the paratroopers and jumped into the back. The truck continued up and down the street until it was full and then sped out U.S. 95 toward camp.

About 11:30 that night Newsome awoke in a drunken fog, his head comfortably resting on the bosom of his new friend. He looked at his watch and turned to gently nudge the sleeping girl. Convincing her to drive him to the Golden Nugget, he reached the club by midnight, only to find that Dann and the rest of the paratroopers were long gone. Graciously, the girl agreed to drive him all the way back to camp.

The HumRRO psychologists had been thwarted once again by Smoky. They still didn't know how well the men would perform their assigned tasks after witnessing their first nuclear blast. Fallout precluded using either the Smoky obstacle course or the newly prepared Wheeler course after Smoky. But while the paratroopers were whooping it up in Las Vegas, the HumRRO team members got their first break of the Plumbbob series — the AEC moved up the scheduled blast of Galileo by 24 hours.

Newsome darted into the Quonset hut as Dann and the others were strapping on their pistol belts. Waving to Dann with a lascivious wink and a grin, he rushed to change into his fatigues. By 1:30 A.M. the paratroopers were climbing aboard the trucks once again for the ride to Yucca Flat. Dann, Newsome and Hamberger were there, along with Lieutenant Ginn and 76 other soldiers. Cooper was already back at Fort Bragg. Donald Coe was on his way to yet another trench, about five miles from the bomb.

The wind was blowing at 14 knots when Dann and the others marched from their trucks to a flat expanse of desert only about two and a half miles west of ground zero. Some of the men gathered sagebrush and grease-wood and lit fires to take the chill out of the air. The HumRRO scientists took a head count and realized that 19 of the 99 paratroopers scheduled for the test had failed to return from Las Vegas. Again the psychologists were forced to change their plans and reorganize the squads for the tests.

There hadn't been any time to bulldoze any new trenches or to clear an area for the rifle test. They decided that the squads would just have to do their best to find small clearings. The HumRRO team was now down to only three scientists and a few assistant monitors. They divided the men into six squads and announced that only one rifle test would be made, one minute after the blast. The paratroopers were ordered to hunker down in the open and wait for the explosion.

At 5:40 A.M., Galileo, an 11kt bomb, was detonated. When the shock wave passed over the huddled troops, one of the HumRRO researchers blew his whistle and the rifle test began. Only a few of the men bothered to disassemble their rifles in the heavy dust. The rest stood around mumbling about all the radiation safety regulations that had been violated. As Dann recalled later, "All they wanted to see was whether we'd walk around with our heads up our asses or puke and fall down."

Newsome field-stripped his rifle absent-mindedly. After all the practice in the previous weeks, he could have done it with his eyes closed.

As it was, his eyes were wide open. He was spellbound by the Galileo fireball rising to its zenith. "It was the clearest light I'd ever seen," Newsome remembered. "If there was a lizard on a rock 20 miles away, I think I could have seen him."

All Hamberger could think about was how hungry he was. He hadn't had anything to eat since noon the day before, and the rumbling in his stomach was competing with the sound of the bomb blast across the flat.

The HumRRO psychologists reported that the soldiers' rifle-stripping proficiency was "reduced by the blast." Because the troopers used at the Galileo shot were already veterans of a previous atomic shot, the data the researchers gathered that day were useless and the experiment with the green-clad guinea pigs was inconclusive.

The troopers' previous exposure at Smoky "blew our scientific model," said HumRRO team leader Shep Schwartz. "The validity of the experiment went right down the drain. The attitude of the soldiers and the other scientists was pretty much like mine — go ahead and get it over with. They weren't going to be impressed with anything at that point. But we were affected to a certain degree by Army tenacity. You know, you gotta carry out your mission!"

After the completion of the rifle test, one of the HumRRO team members and an Army radiation monitor drove to the Smoky crawling course in a jeep to see if the area could be safely entered. The paratroopers waited by the trucks, munching on assault rations. The two scouts returned about 7:00 A.M. and announced that the course could be used if the soldiers didn't tarry in the area for more than an hour.

A radiological safety officer briefed the troops, telling them to be especially careful while in the Smoky area. Several of the soldiers, Newsome among them, boarded one of the trucks and were driven to the crawling course.

They scrambled beneath the barbed-wire fences, jumped in the fox-holes and threw the grenades, just as they'd been taught. Then the troopers marched at a rout step toward the Smoky ground zero. The hill behind the tower, once covered with Joshua trees and Yucca plants, was now barren and devoid of any color except the scorched brown earth. The vicinity of the tower was surrealistic, with the look of a motionless moonscape.

Newsome wandered across the sandy flat, brushing up against a creosote bush when he tripped over a rock hidden beneath the loose earth.

A radiation monitor scampered over and waved his instrument in an arc across Newsome's body.

"You're real hot, corporal," the monitor said excitedly. "Be sure and get on that bus back at the trucks. You gotta go to Camp Mercury for decontamination."

Unperturbed, Newsome promised to follow the monitor's instructions and walked back toward the crawling course at a leisurely pace. By 8:55 the paratroopers were all on their way to Camp Desert Rock.

Newsome and a few others, including Private Robert Schaudenecker, the former Chicago fireman, rode to Camp Mercury on a bus. At the gate, a guard walked up the aisle, checking the soldiers' identification tags against a master roster. Security at the AEC installation was extraordinarily tight.

The contaminated soldiers were ordered to strip and shower. Radiation technicians passed Geiger counters over their bodies repeatedly. Newsome and Schaudenecker were told to shower for a second time. A doctor recorded their pulse rates, temperatures and heart rates and took blood samples. They were given new clothing and sent along to Camp Desert Rock after the AEC doctors offered convincing assurances that they were both all right. The careful decontamination effort, the doctors explained earnestly, was only a precaution.

Dann eagerly bought a copy of the Las Vegas *Sun* the next morning when he saw a headline on the paper's front page that said: " 'GALILEO' JOLTS PARATROOPERS IN TEST SITE MANEUVERS." But when he read through the article, Dann was revolted by the disparity between what he knew to be the truth and the hyperbolic newspaper description of the previous day's happenings.

It wasn't the reporter's fault. He could only report what he was told, Dann thought. The article began honestly enough. It explained that the troopers were in the field for a test of their "nerve survival potential." That was true, as far as Dann knew.

The reporter was also correct in noting that the paratroopers of the 82nd were the first American soldiers "to bear the shock of an atomic explosion so close on an open battlefield without the protection of trench walls or concrete or steel shelters to minimize the fearsome heat and shock waves." But when Dann followed the story's jump to one of the back pages of the newspaper and read the comments of the HumRRO team leader, he began seething with rage.

"The answer to how steely-nerved American paratroopers are under nuclear fire," the story continued, "came in preliminary evaluation statements issued by Shepard G. Schwartz, a sociologist of Alexandria, Va. . . . 'They reacted very calmly and seemingly carried out their functions normally,' said Schwartz."

"Steely-nerved. Calm. Normal. What a bunch of bull," Dann muttered to no one in particular. He crumpled the newspaper into a ball and tossed it into the trash. Silently, he packed his gear for the trip home.

The next morning the paratroopers were back at Indian Springs Air Force Base, loading onto another Globemaster for the flight to North Carolina. The plane lifted into the air and banked sharply southward, cruising over Lake Mead and Hoover Dam. The pilots weren't taking the paratroopers on a joy ride, they simply needed to gain enough speed and altitude to clear the high mountains east of the landing strip.

As the plane climbed upward, the soldiers let out a collective cheer. None of the paratroopers seemed to be too deeply saddened to leave the Spartan amenities offered by Camp Desert Rock.

"We made it, Danny-boy," Newsome exulted when the plane flew over the mountain peaks.

"You betcha we made it, Chuck. Couldn't'a happened any other way." Dann heaved a sigh of relief and grinned broadly at Hamberger, who already was warming up his dice for another marathon crap game.

What Russell Jack Dann didn't know as he contentedly lit up a cigarette was that he was destined to spend the rest of his life with the mushroom-shaped specter of Smoky poised above him.

For Russell Dann and the other members of Task Force Big Bang, their days as atomic soldiers had ended. In fact, Operation Plumbbob also marked the finale of large-scale participation by troops in atomic-bomb maneuvers. Yet only the locale changed. The exposure of American servicemen to the bombs' effects continued unabated in the Marshall Islands in the distant South Pacific.

Within a month after Operation Plumbbob drew to a close, U.S. scientists were on their way to Eniwetok atoll to begin preparations for Operation Hardtack, another series of nuclear bomb tests.

The natives of Eniwetok had lived undisturbed on their atoll for centuries, developing sophisticated skills as navigators, canoe builders and fishermen. Bright and ingenious, they adapted easily to the customs and traditions of a succession of colonial traders and missionaries who landed on the atoll, while fiercely maintaining their own individualistic identity. All that changed in mid-February 1945.

A combined force of Army infantrymen and U.S. Marines assaulted the Japanese garrison occupying the atoll. After three days of savage fighting in the thick, mosquito-infested jungle, the U.S. forces had suffered only 131 casualties while taking a toll of 700 dead enemy soldiers. Only two dozen of the island's defenders allowed themselves to be taken prisoner. For the Americans, it was an important victory in the island-hopping campaign toward Japan. But for the people of Eniwetok, only the skin color of the new colonials had changed. The atoll was still occupied.

Still, the Americans were more benevolent masters. The islands had been virtually devastated by warfare. The U.S. Navy resettled all of the 120-some people of the atoll in a small compact village on Aomon Island. Because of a rivalry between two tribal chiefs, the islanders shortly afterward moved again to Bijire Island, which was under the authority of the more popular chief. Ultimately the choice of where the Eniwetok people would live was decided in Washington.

The United States wanted to use the atoll for nuclear testing. Again, the harried islanders were forced to pack up their belongings and move to Meik Island in the Kwajalein atoll. A short time later they were relocated once more to Ujelang atoll, a land mass one-quarter the size of Eniwetok 124 miles to the southwest.

During the decade between 1948 and 1958, Eniwetok was the scene of 43 nuclear detonations. Twenty-three nuclear blasts also erupted on the nearby Bikini atoll during that period. Most of the tests, except one, were uneventful. The AEC scientists did make one notable error at the test of an experimental thermonuclear device on Bikini in February 1954.

The yield of the 15-megaton bomb was badly miscalculated. Fallout from the explosion was carried far beyond the "danger area" that the scientists estimated the radiation would reach. All of the 64 residents of Rongelap atoll were heavily contaminated and had to be evacuated. They were unable to return until years later. The cloud also dumped "Bikini ash" on the Japanese fishing trawler *Fukuryu Maru* (Lucky Dragon), which was netting tuna 80 miles to the east. The 25 crew members of the vessel suffered radiation sickness, and one died seven months later from the effects of the poisoning.

The fallout was a stiff blow to the Japanese fishing industry. More than a million pounds of sea life were seized by the government and destroyed. Among the 64 Rongelap islanders exposed, one woman contracted thyroid cancer and several of the children suffered from serious growth retardation. The U.S. government was quick to offer compensation to the islanders and the *Fukuryu Maru* crew to stem the groundswell of protest both in the United States and in Japan.

For 360 days, starting in November 1957, Army Sergeant Orville Kelly called the white-sanded beaches of Japtan Island in the Eniwetok atoll home. He was the noncommissioned officer in charge of an inter-service squad of men assigned to the isle for Operation Hardtack. The first few months on the island, known in Army records as "Site David," were idyllic for Kelly and the men under his command. They fished the abundant sea and swam in the crystal blue lagoon surrounded by the 30 small islands dotting the atoll. The land area on all the islets totaled a mere two and a half square miles. The highest ground was only 13 feet above the sea. To the Americans, Eniwetok was a tropical paradise.

As island commander, it was Kelly's job to record measurements of radiation at various locations on Japtan where pools of water were present. He used a Geiger counter and reported the measurements to his superiors by radio. It was also Kelly's duty to muster the men under his command to watch each of the blasts.

The soldiers and sailors would gather before dawn at the lagoon side of the island nearest the blast centers and don protective goggles. Without exception, they were ordered to face all the blasts and watch the rising mushroom clouds five miles away.

There were problems. Many of the men didn't want to watch the explosions. They wanted off the island — desperately. Kelly represented authority and hence became the target of his subordinates' hostility. When one Navy petty officer had a bit too much to drink the night before a test, he told Kelly he'd kill him if he was forced to watch another shot. Everyone was scared. Things were getting out of control. Tension on Japtan Island seemed to electrify the air itself.

The men assigned to Site David witnessed 22 separate nuclear blasts during Operation Hardtack. For many, the bombs left deep psychological scars. At one point, Kelly himself complained to a board of officers about the morale problems on the island and requested a transfer.

"I told them I just couldn't control things anymore," the sergeant recalled. "The men were scared and anxious. So was I. I wanted to be replaced, but they just told me I was doing a great job and to get back to my island. I wasn't coaxed, I was ordered.''

While inspecting a wrecked ship in the lagoon offshore, Kelly slipped and the knifelike shards of the coral reef sliced deeply into his legs. Bleeding profusely, he had to wade through about 400 yards of the contaminated sea to reach his island. For days, the wounds festered and bled.

''I spent several days in my Quonset hut before summoning an M-boat to take me to the dispensary,'' said the former Army sergeant 20 years later. ''Meanwhile, the wounds on my legs had become infected. But I was returned to duty before the wounds had healed because they considered my assignment critical. In fact, they hadn't even healed completely by the time I left the Army two years later.''

When Kelly continued to complain about the problems on the island, a medical officer was dispatched to Japtan for a consultation.

''We talked,'' said Kelly. ''I told him about my problems and my fears. He seemed to be interested and concerned. On the next boat of supplies, a bottle of phenobarbital arrived. Apparently they thought that sedatives would solve all the problems on Japtan.''

After nearly a year on the island, Kelly's film badge recorded a dose of only 3.4 roentgens of gamma radiation.

Dr. Karl Z. Morgan, the AEC's foremost expert on the health effects of radiation, was also in the South Pacific during Operation Hardtack. Known as the ''father of the science of health physics,'' Morgan had an association with atomic testing dating back to the Manhattan Project. He pioneered the radiation health effects field, served as editor of the respected *Health Physics* medical journal and in 1958 was director of health physics at the government's Oak Ridge, Tennessee, National Laboratory.

During Hardtack, Morgan complained that the film badges and portable survey meters being used to evaluate the radiation doses on Eniwetok were clearly inadequate. He was given a crew of men to conduct better measurements and immediately set off to get a more accurate picture of the radiation doses the test participants were being exposed to.

Today, the tall, white-haired Morgan is still treated deferentially by his fellow scientists. They know his accomplishments well. Now Neely professor of physics at Georgia Institute of Technology, the soft-spoken patrician-looking scientist still recalls the events of Operation Hardtack with clarity.

"The film badges and survey meters in use by the military during those tests," Morgan remembers, "gave essentially zero response to the beta dose. And the beta dose was about three times as high as the gamma dose. In some places, for example on the ships, the beta-emitting radio-nucleides were absorbed into the paint and tar resins so that the beta dose was 600 times the gamma dose. It was so hot down below, the sailors would sleep out on the decks and they'd wake up with erythema — sunburns that weren't from the sun. The burns were from beta radiation."

Morgan wrote several papers about his findings, but, as usual, whenever scientific evidence was proffered that differed from the official government line, the evidence was ignored. However, in the succeeding months, the fallout concerns of a host of scientists grew ever stronger — too strong to ignore.

7

SCIENCE VERSUS SCIENCE

The quantum leaps made by the scientists of the Manhattan Project captured the imagination of the American public after World War II. Shy, unassuming researchers who had spent the bulk of their lives laboring in anonymity suddenly found themselves thrust into the public eye, the objects of adoration and reverence. In their search for keys to unlocking nature's mysteries, the scientists had discarded petty partisan disagreements: the importance of their goal transcended politics. One veteran of the effort even referred to his scientific colleagues as a "new priesthood."

While politics could not put asunder the unity of the atomic savants, within a few short years after the monumental successes of the war the "priesthood" was deeply split over questions about the long-term health effects of low-level radiation. Old alliances and friendships were forgotten as the scientists divided into opposing camps, each side struggling to make its philosophy reign supreme. The disagreement quickly grew into an intellectual abyss that has yet to be bridged.

By 1958 the nation was enmeshed in a protracted debate over whether the United States should develop so-called clean bombs that would destroy potential enemies without spreading dangerous fallout. In the midst of the controversy, Dr. Edward Teller told a Senate subcommittee that if the U.S. ended its atmospheric bomb tests in Nevada, millions would be killed in any future atomic war because America's foes were certain to capitalize on any timidity shown by the United States.

The AEC commissioners agreed with Teller for a variety of reasons. According to the secret minutes of their meeting on November 14, Dr. Willard Libby went on the record opposing the clean bombs because "there was a desire by the military for some degree of off-site radiation for troop training purposes."

Commissioner John McCone suggested conducting all future tests underground, but Libby argued that while the safer underground blasts wouldn't interfere with the AEC's bomb development program, it could "impair the Defense Department's training program." In the end, the commissioners decided that the best course of action was no action at all. They concluded that the AEC "should not propose at this time, a unilateral self-imposed limitation on testing."

Phase II of Operation Hardtack began at the Nevada Test Site in September. By the time the series was over on October 30, 18 more bombs had been detonated, mostly above ground. The Soviets too were continuing to explode nuclear devices by the dozen in Siberia. The Naval Research Laboratory measured a 300 percent increase in the amount of atmospheric radioactivity by the time all the testing came to a halt.

Nobel Prize–winner Dr. Linus Pauling was stumping the country again, warning that radioactive carbon 14 already left in the air would lead to five million genetically defective births and millions of cancer and leukemia deaths in the succeeding 300 generations.

In Russia, the Kremlin leaders were under similar pressures from their own scientists to put a stop to the testing. Another Nobel Prize–winner, physicist Andrei Sakharov, warned Soviet Premier Nikita Khrushchev that for every megaton of fissionable material exploded in the atmosphere, 10,000 people would die of cancer. Both the United States and the U.S.S.R. unofficially agreed to stop detonating atomic bombs in the atmosphere and the testing went underground temporarily. The rivalry between the two nations moved to a new arena — space.

On October 4, 1957, the Soviet Union successfully launched the first man-made moon, a satellite known as *Sputnik I*. The race for space was on, and American officials were determined not to fall behind. An intensive program began to develop bigger, more powerful intercontinental ballistic missiles capable of carrying not only nuclear warheads, but satellites as well. Less than two weeks after the Russian success, the United States was able to fire two aluminum pellets into space, and after several failures the first U.S. earth satellite, *Explorer,* blasted off from Cape Canaveral on January 31, 1958.

The United States also was embroiled in a contest between the East and West over which nation would be first to put the atom to peaceful use. Five and a half years before, President Eisenhower had surprised the world by boldly proposing before the United Nations General Assembly that the nations then undertaking large atomic projects pool their fissionable materials and distribute a portion to other countries for peaceful uses. Eisenhower suggested that in the hands of scientists and engineers these materials could help scientific research and medicine. He contended that atoms might also be used to produce electricity.

Until that time most research in atomic energy was carried out in great secrecy. The majority of the world's populace never conceived that the atom could be used for anything but terror and destruction. Eisenhower's proposal was dubbed the "Atoms-for-Peace Plan."

At Eisenhower's suggestion, the United Nations sponsored the first International Conference on the Peaceful Uses of Atomic Energy in Geneva, Switzerland, during the summer of 1955. For the first time, atomic scientists from behind the Iron Curtain met with their counterparts from the West. In all, 1,400 scientists and government representatives from 73 countries participated in the conference. The Russians had already started successfully generating electricity from an atomic reactor in June 1954, and they proudly showed off color photos and charts of their accomplishments in Geneva.

By October 1956 the world's second atomic power plant went into operation at Calder Hall in England. It was officially inaugurated by Queen Elizabeth. When the queen pulled a switch, electricity from the plant flowed into the power lines. Not to be outdone, in May' 1958 President Eisenhower sent an electric impulse to Shippingport, Pennsylvania, opening a valve and sending electricity from America's first commercial atomic power plant to Pittsburgh, about 30 miles away.

The Shippingport plant, designed and developed as an experimental reactor by Navy Admiral Hyman Rickover and funded jointly by the AEC and the Duquesne Light Company, generated 60,000 kilowatts of power — more than either the Russian or British reactors. A much larger plant went on-line two years later at Dresden, Illinois, 50 miles southwest of Chicago, generating 180,000 kilowatts. Eisenhower's dream of "Atoms for Peace" had become a reality.

Still, the feelings of a growing number of scientists toward the damage that had already been done by atomic-bomb fallout were anything but peaceful. In 1959, the Joint Committee on Atomic Energy again held hearings on the fallout question.

Dr. Jack Schubert, a radiobiologist from the government's Argonne National Laboratory in Chicago, testified that radiation from nuclear tests and from medical X-rays could indeed be hazardous. He cited the pioneering research of British scientist Dr. Alice Stewart, an Oxford University epidemiologist who the year before had published a paper which showed that women who were X-rayed while pregnant gave birth to children who had a much greater chance of contracting and dying of childhood leukemia than others who were not exposed to radiation.

Schubert's testimony was unprecedented. After all, here was an AEC scientist saying essentially the same thing that opponents to atomic testing were saying and providing evidence to support his contentions. For his trouble, Schubert was pilloried by his fellows.

However, his testimony did have far-reaching results: it captivated a Westinghouse Electric Corporation radiological physics researcher named Dr. Ernest Sternglass and sent him on a quest to learn more about the relationship between X-ray radiation and its health effects. Sternglass surmised that if a single dose of radiation from an X-ray would give rise to cancer and leukemia, an equally low dose from fallout spread over a long period of time might well have the same effect.

In the fall of 1961 the Soviets broke the voluntarily imposed atmospheric test ban treaty by exploding several large nuclear devices in Siberia. The following spring the United States responded by exploding bombs and nuclear missiles of its own in Nevada, the Pacific and the Christmas Island area. The testing continued in earnest throughout the year. Nuclear brinksmanship had become, once again, a persuasive instrument of U.S. strategic policy as the cold war with Russia heated up.

While the world's superpowers postured, the animated, bespectacled Sternglass was hard at work in his Westinghouse laboratory in Pittsburgh. By 1962, he had found what he thought would at last prove true the theories of Linus Pauling and E. B. Lewis.

Six years earlier, the AEC had successfully fended off Pauling's assertion that fallout was a factor in increased cancer and leukemia rates by contending that the chemist's extrapolations of high radiation dose effects to low dose effects weren't valid and couldn't be proved. But Sternglass had carefully studied the research done by Alice Stewart on the effects of one-roentgen X-ray radiation on fetuses. Sternglass also perused the findings of Harvard epidemiologist Dr. Brian MacMahon, whose own studies confirmed Stewart's research.

He analyzed the two studies and corrected Stewart's data to conform to the results MacMahon found at even lower X-ray doses. The professor knew he had a bombshell in his hands. For years the AEC had contended that there was a threshold of radiation exposure that would have to be reached before any somatic effects would show up. But Sternglass' analysis showed there was a direct, "linear" relationship between low doses of radiation and childhood cancer. Thus, a dose of one roentgen given in the course of a one-hour series of X-ray pictures could be regarded as producing essentially the same effect as one thousandth of a roentgen per hour from fallout over a period of 1,000 hours.

In October 1962 Sternglass flew to Washington to consult with Dr. Ralph Lapp on his analysis. Lapp had published a widely read book called *The Voyage of the Lucky Dragon* about the Bikini ash fallout of 1954 and was a renowned expert on fallout effects. At the time he was serving as a special consultant to the White House. President John F. Kennedy was facing a tough test by the Russians. The Soviets had stationed offensive nuclear missiles in Cuba, and the massive atomic arsenals of both nations bristled in readiness. Lapp was providing the White House with a realistic appraisal of what nuclear war would cost in human lives.

Sternglass arrived at Lapp's office on October 21. Spread out over the physicist's desk were aerial photos of Russian missile silos in Cuba. Lapp, though preoccupied by thoughts of possible war and disaster, graciously went over Sternglass' theories with him, making corrections and offering suggestions. Then, turning to his friend, Lapp explained that Kennedy was going to announce a naval and air "quarantine" of Cuba the next evening. "I'm going home now, Ernest," Lapp said nervously, "to my bomb shelter."

Sternglass submitted a paper on his research to *Science* magazine, but it was rejected. According to the magazine's editor, Dr. Philip Abelson, the paper had been harshly criticized by one of two reviewers who considered it unworthy of publication. It so happened that Abelson was a close friend of the new AEC chairman, Dr. Glenn Seaborg. Often when he received a submission to *Science* on radiation or fallout, Abelson would send it off for a critique by AEC scientists. Invariably, the papers would go unpublished after unfavorable critiques were lodged by the "reputable" AEC staff.

Abelson was also serving as a member of the Plowshare Committee, a group of advisers to the AEC on peaceful applications of atomic devices. Like many physicists repulsed by the horrifying uses atomic fission was being put to, the Plowshare scientists were determined to prove that the atom could be used for good as well as evil. They conceived of using atomic bombs to help mine coal, release natural gas deposits, dig canals and divert rivers. Though several experimental bombs were detonated in Nevada as part of the Plowshare program, none was ever actually put to use.

Sternglass knew that Abelson's association with Seaborg and the AEC was working against him, so he began seeking support. Armed with endorsements of his paper by Lapp, Johns Hopkins' Dr. Russell Morgan and Dr. Barry Commoner of Washington University in St. Louis, Missouri, Sternglass submitted his paper once again. Under pressure, Abelson acquiesced and the paper was published in the June 1963 issue of *Science*.

Early that summer, President Kennedy realized that the issue of fallout could serve as the fuel for some excellent political mileage. His wife, Jacqueline, was then pregnant with their third child, and Kennedy himself had an understanding of the threat concerned scientists claimed fallout posed to unborn life. In a widely acclaimed speech in Salt Lake City, Kennedy announced that he planned to push for an official ban on atmospheric testing.

The AEC commissioners found themselves between a rock and a hard place. More and more scientists were joining the fold in opposition to bomb testing and the ever-growing capital investment in costly nuclear power generating plants. Though the commissioners were able to do a creditable job in defusing many of the contentions of Pauling, Sternglass, Lewis and other critics by pointing to the fact that these "dissidents" had no empirical proof to bolster their theories, government scientists slowly came to the realization that they had no proof to support their reassurances of safety either.

In late 1962, Dr. John Gofman, who eight years earlier had successfully countered Pauling's allegations on the fallout hazard, was again tapped by the AEC to turn his attention to proving that low levels of radiation were harmless. The approach to Gofman by Dr. John Foster, then the director of the Lawrence Radiation Laboratory in Livermore, California, was both enticing and blunt.

"Look, John," Foster said according to Gofman's recollection, "the AEC commissioners are on the hot seat because we clobbered Utah during the 1961–1962 test series. They're getting all kinds of flak about fallout. Now if we had biologists and medical experts studying this, we wouldn't be getting all this flak.''

Gofman was offered a fully equipped laboratory, a staff of 125 to 150, including 35 senior scientists, and an annual budget ranging from three to three-and-a-half million dollars. It was an offer he could not refuse.

Gofman and his associate, Dr. Arthur Tamplin, were given a broad mandate. Their study was to quantify the impact on man and the biosphere of radiation and radionucleides from all man-made activities, including bomb testing, medical research, the Plowshare program and nuclear power generation. Never in history had such a comprehensive study of radiation's effects been undertaken.

On July 25, after only ten days of intensive negotiations in Moscow, representatives of the United States, Great Britain and the U.S.S.R. initialed a treaty banning any further testing of nuclear weapons in the atmosphere. The signing was hailed around the world as a great victory for the opponents of nuclear weapons. But the cessation of atmospheric testing did not quell the debate over what damage might already have been wrought by the bombs or what effects were yet to be seen by America's headlong rush to make nuclear power the new "god of energy."

The hot debate generated by the test ban treaty, the publication of Sternglass' paper, the Gofman-Tamplin research project and the rising tide of public concern about the long-term legacy of the bomb testing gave a renewed impetus to the fallout furor. Another set of hearings on the issue was convened by the Joint Committee only weeks before the treaty was initialed. Testimony continued throughout the summer.

The banter between the members of the committee and the AEC and other government witnesses called to testify was heated. The congressmen concentrated on three known facts: First, no standards whatsoever had ever been developed for fallout radiation. Second, the government had lagged in developing any countermeasures to protect the public. And finally, no agency of the government kept the public informed of possible hazards. In contrast, the AEC had done its utmost to deny any danger.

Several government witnesses were able to downplay the committee's concerns. Dr. Paul Tompkins, for instance, then the director of the Federal Radiation Council and the man empowered to set standards for public exposure to radiation, argued that guidelines had never been established for fallout because standards already existed governing the actions of public health officials when the public health and safety was threatened by any sort of radiation.

The taciturn Tompkins disputed the contention that the government had lagged behind in developing countermeasures, saying that "up to the present time, the government has judged that the need for wide-scale activities of this kind does not exist." Tompkins also cited several federal publications available to the public that listed radiation measurements.

A host of government scientists and researchers paraded before the committee to deny that they had been lax. They pointed to the various bureaucratic organizations that were working to impose radiation standards and countermeasures and presented the newly awarded research grant to Gofman as evidence that their efforts to get a handle on the "possible" fallout hazard were well motivated and sincere.

The civilized give-and-take between the committee members and the government witnesses was disrupted on June 7 by the introduction of a statement by the Pittsburgh chapter of the Federation of American Scientists on links between low-level radiation and childhood cancer.

Based on the *Science* article written by Sternglass, the federation charged that fallout from the U.S. and U.S.S.R. testing of the year before would certainly lead to a 2.5–10 percent increase in normal childhood cancer mortality in the United States. The statement predicted that 100 to 400 American children already had been doomed to death by the fallout that year, a toll roughly comparable to the number of people who died of polio in the nation during 1960.

Dr. Charles Dunham, director of the AEC's Division of Biology and Medicine, quickly refuted the charge with a detailed critique of Sternglass' paper, and the work of Stewart and MacMahon, from which the Pittsburgh scientist had drawn his data. Dunham accused Sternglass of glaring inaccuracies in his calculations and assumptions based not on fact but theory. While the AEC admitted that research in the area was needed and noted that efforts to quantify the hazard were then underway, Dunham concluded his parry of Sternglass' charges by saying that it was "difficult to ascribe any confidence whatever" to the professor's arguments.

When hearings before the committee reconvened in August, Dr. Shields Warren, the "conscience of the AEC" when that body was debating the pros and cons of allowing military observers to move to positions close to the atomic-bomb blasts, came to the defense of his scientific colleagues in government. Warren testified that Tompkins' Federal Radiation Council would be an "ideal" agency to develop guidelines limiting public exposure to radiation.

Warren recommended taking the lowest level of exposure at which harm was known to occur in man and apply a reasonable safety factor to limit exposure below that level. "My memory," said Warren, "is that the lowest level, if we are talking about thyroid, at which positive harm has been done — and this dosage is somewhat in question — is in the order of 100 roentgens."

Laboratory tests had proved that the thyroid gland of infants and children was most susceptible to physiological changes after exposure to radiation. Most of those changes involved cancers on the gland. Warren argued that by setting guidelines for various radio isotopes, like strontium 90 and iodine 131, contaminated milk could be dumped and the population limited to consuming stored food.

The August hearings before the Joint Committee were unusual if only for the fact that the long line of witnesses was not confined to those sycophants of the AEC who mimicked the government line. In fact, a chorus of critics was called before the committee to present the other side of the radiation controversy.

Dr. E. B. Lewis of the California Institute of Technology had decried the dangers of fallout and strontium 90 years before. At the August hearings, Lewis explained that he had just completed a study of medical radiologists and the effect their work with X-rays had on their health. Lewis found that the radiologists died of leukemia at a rate three times higher than normal. "A statistically highly significant excess of deaths occurred," he testified. Lewis' study also revealed a death rate among the radiologists from multiple myeloma, cancer of the bone marrow, that was five times the norm.

The medical community was under attack for unnecessarily exposing patients and radiation technicians to dangerous amounts of radiation. Much of the problem stemmed from outmoded X-ray machines that exposed patients and operators to more than twice the amount of radiation needed to produce an image on the X-ray film. Other overexposures were a matter of economy. X-ray machines always have been extraordinarily expensive, yet a doctor who had one in his office was considered special. Consequently, doctors often used X-rays for simple diagnostic procedures to impress their patients and amortize the cost of the machines.

X-ray treatments were used for everything from examining fractures to treatment of adolescent acne. Many large department stores had fluoroscopes in their shoe departments. It was an exciting treat for schoolchildren in the 1950s to visit the shoe store, stand on the machines and wonder at the sight of their own footbones. Dr. Karl Z. Morgan was one of the first scientists to recognize the folly and the danger of excessive radiation exposure from medical procedures.

In the early 1950s he launched an attack on the American Medical Association and the Radiological Society of North America, charging that the abuse of X-rays could and should be stopped. As a physicist, Morgan knew that by adding filters, columnizing the X-ray beams into a smaller area and controlling the development process so several exposures wouldn't be necessary to get one good picture, the problem could be drastically reduced.

The scientist's attack backfired. He succeeded only in arousing the ire and the defensive instincts of the medical community. Whenever Morgan made a statement on unnecessary exposures, a dozen radiologists would counter his arguments. And by 1963, even though E. B. Lewis had evidence that the radiologists were killing themselves, the medical community successfuly resisted any regulation with charges that the government was about to turn America's country doctors into socialized medical practitioners.

Harvard University epidemiologist Dr. Brian MacMahon also testified before the Joint Committee that summer. He told the members that his studies, confirming the earlier work of Oxford's Dr. Alice Stewart, showed that children who had been exposed to radiation below the two-roentgen range while in their mothers' wombs had a cancer risk "in the first ten years of life about 40 percent higher than children who had not been exposed."

Dr. Eric Reiss, a member of the St. Louis Citizens' Committee for Nuclear Information and an associate professor of medicine at that city's Washington University, also testified. Reiss pointed out that his analysis of the AEC's own radiation monitoring reports in Nevada and Utah showed that "a number of local populations . . . have been exposed to fallout so intense as to represent a medically unacceptable hazard to children who may drink fresh locally produced milk." Shot Smoky, said Reiss, "delivered an estimated 10 to 67 roentgens over an 8,000-square-mile area outside the Nevada Test Site. The local fallout pattern from that shot spread significant doses as far as 700 miles north to Rock Springs, Wyoming.''

Reiss also noted that the amount of iodine 131 in the milk tested near the Nevada Test Site was at levels even the Federal Radiation Council considered carcinogenic, yet no action was taken to limit consumption of the contaminated liquid. Only once, in all the years of testing, said Reiss, was locally produced milk diverted and uncontaminated milk brought to Utah to avoid a radiation hazard. And that was in the summer of 1962, at the end of atmospheric nuclear testing.

Finally, on August 22, Dr. Ernest Sternglass was given an opportunity to defend himself, and his theories, before the committee. In the two months since the publication of his paper in *Science*, Sternglass had been the subject of scorn and vilification within the government scientific community. In an unprecedented attempt to blunt the sharp Sternglass allegations, the AEC had successfully managed to plant harsh newspaper stories across the country belittling the professor's work and saddling him with the derisive sobriquet "Prophet of Doom."

Sternglass began his testimony with an assault on the scientific community's prevailing wisdom: that a threshold level of radiation had to be reached before any deleterious effects were seen.

"I believe," Sternglass declared, "that the combined evidence independently gathered by Dr. MacMahon and Dr. Stewart provides for the first time conclusive evidence that there is indeed no threshold for the production of serious somatic effects, such as leukemia, larger than the dose from a single pelvic X-ray picture in the 200 to 400 milliroentgen range. This," the professor declared pointedly, "I believe to be the single most important and most definite conclusion that can be drawn from existing data. Thus, there is no longer a need to extrapolate from very high total doses."

"Overinquisitive radiology and unnecessary exposure to any form of radiation" — Sternglass paused dramatically — "cannot be too strongly condemned." Under cross-examination by the committee members, the scientist amplified his testimony. He said only a single "hit" or dose of a small amount of radiation on a vital part of a human's cell structure was sufficient to ultimately produce the possibility of cancer resulting from that exposure.

Sternglass, MacMahon, Reiss and the other scientists who subscribed to the "linear" hypothesis of dose response left the committee hearings thinking they had scored a major victory. They had recommended that the government immediately sponsor research in the area, and, in fact, later that month the Joint Committee asked the surgeon general to begin a study of cancer mortality rates in Utah, Nevada, Arizona and other states that were heavily contaminated with fallout during bomb testing. Dr. Edward Weiss of the Bureau of Radiological Health immediately began work on the project.

Only a few short months after the Joint Committee hearings, the Federal Radiation Council under Dr. Paul Tompkins finally took some action on creating guidelines to protect the public. Yet the action he took was not in any way what Sternglass, MacMahon, Lewis and other critics envisioned. When radioactive iodine 131 was discovered in milk at levels higher than had ever been measured before, the Council secretly decided to raise the acceptable limits of radio iodine in milk threefold. The move meant that public health officials would not have to remove contaminated milk from the market even if extraordinarily high amounts of radiation were found in it.

The next year, the AEC also began funding a research project by University of Pittsburgh epidemiologist Dr. Thomas Mancuso that was designed to determine whether the exposure of workers at government nuclear facilities led to increased cancer or leukemia rates among them. At the time, Mancuso was one of the world's leading authorities on industrial cancer research. He had achieved international recognition for his discoveries that cancer was prevalent enough to be considered an occupational disease in the asbestos, rubber and petrochemical industries.

Dr. Weiss of the Bureau of Radiological Health was the first to complete his work on radiation effects. However, the results of his research will probably never be known, since much of the data were destroyed. When Weiss tabulated his statistics in 1965 and found marked increases in the thyroid cancer rate among children exposed to fallout in Utah, the paper he prepared explaining his findings was unceremoniously suppressed by the AEC. According to internal documents unearthed 14 years later, the AEC commissioners were worried that if news of Weiss's findings leaked out, the future of nuclear power development in the United States would be "jeopardized."

Also in 1965, Gofman and Tamplin completed the first part of their omnibus study on radiation effects. They concluded that the government's Plowshare program, an attempt to put nuclear bombs to peaceful use by digging a new Panama Canal with 315 megatons of hydrogen bombs, was "biological insanity." The Plowshare program was winding down anyway, and their revelations created barely a ripple within the scientific community. The same cannot be said for the uproar touched off four years later when Gofman and Tamplin completed the bulk of their research.

Gofman's name and prestige had been used in 1957 to blunt the criticisms of Linus Pauling. Besides serving as an AEC shill, the underlying purpose of Gofman's massive research project was to finally provide the government with a credible scientific study that could be used to convince the public that people like Sternglass and Pauling were crackpots. Yet as the years wore on, Gofman's research led him to agree, rather than disagree, with the AEC critics. In fact, he came to realize that Sternglass' death estimates had been too conservative.

In 1969, the most pessimistic prediction by the International Commission on Radiological Protection estimated that for every leukemia induced by radiation, another type of cancer would also be caused. That year, when Gofman and Tamplin finished their work, they found that the effects of low-level radiation had been grossly underestimated by at least 20 times. According to their data, the two scientists predicted that the annual dose of 170 milliroentgens of radiation allowed to the general population was probably causing an extra 32,000 cancers and leukemias every year.

In late November, after Gofman and Tamplin presented their findings, Dr. Michael May, director of the Lawrence Lab, called Gofman to his office to complain about the researchers' public statements. According to Gofman, May accused him of releasing bombshells without first clearing them with the AEC. The two men argued and Gofman adamantly told May that he would not tolerate censorship of his work. May indignantly informed the researcher that he wouldn't allow laboratory work to be censored either, and the two men parted on good terms. "As far as I was concerned," Gofman recalled later, "there was nothing to worry about."

There was plenty to worry about.

Between Christmas and the New Year, Tamplin was scheduled to present a paper on his work before the American Association for the Advancement of Science in Washington. Dutifully, he first sent the paper to his superiors. When the paper was returned, "everything but the prepositions" was deleted.

Dr. Roger Batzel, associate director of the lab, told Tamplin in no uncertain terms that if he insisted on presenting his paper before the AAAS, he was not to use his government-paid secretary to type it and neither his name nor any mention of his affiliation with Livermore could appear on the paper. And the government, said Batzel, would not pay for his travel to Washington.

Gofman was outraged. He called May and asked what the hell was going on. May replied, "For heaven's sake, Jack, be reasonable." But Gofman was so incensed he was beyond reason. The scientist wrote a terse letter to the AAAS, detailing what had happened to Tamplin and labeling the Livermore Lab a "scientific whorehouse." When May learned what Gofman had done, the director relented and Tamplin was allowed to present his paper with only minor modifications. But that wasn't the end of the controversy. Both Gofman and Tamplin had made a strategic mistake — they resisted the will of the AEC and their days of freedom at Livermore were numbered.

Gofman had resigned as director of the laboratory's Division of Biology and Medicine six months before and, with only a skeleton staff, was concentrating on pure research into the effects of radiation on chromosomes. But Tamplin was summarily stripped of 12 of the 13 scientists within his purview and hounded from government. Gofman's punishment came in 1972.

Roger Batzel, Gofman's successor as the director of the Biology and Medicine Division and currently head of the Lawrence Lab, called the bearded scientist into his office and delivered a solemn warning. The AEC, Batzel explained, said the laboratory was overfunded and recommended taking $250,000 from Gofman's chromosome research grant. The scientist managed to stall the inevitable — for a while.

In February 1973 the AEC delivered an ultimatum: either Gofman's $250,000 research grant was eliminated or a quarter of a million dollars would be stripped from the lab's overall funding. Gofman resigned in disgust, his seven-year research project into radiation's chromosomal effects cut short at the height of its productivity. In the end, once the AEC had its blood, no money was ever taken from the laboratory's budget.

The AEC failed in its attempts to stifle Gofman and Tamplin though. Both men became vocal and widely listened to critics of government radiation policy. Tamplin began work with an environmental group, the Natural Resources Defense Council, as a consultant. Gofman joined his old nemesis, Linus Pauling, and became chairman of a group of scientists known as the Committee for Nuclear Responsibility.

Today, Gofman deeply regrets his role in the campaign to discredit Pauling twenty years ago. In 1957, Gofman contended that since Pauling could not prove his allegations of fallout hazard, the AEC should not permit the Nobel Prize winner's concern from interfering with the forward movement of the atomic weapons and energy development program.

"My cardinal error," Gofman says now, "was that I failed to realize a central principle of public health science — in ignorance refrain. My position should have been just the opposite of what I took. If there was no way to disprove Pauling, then the correct approach was to refrain from going ahead with atomic energy until the issue was resolved.

"What I was, in effect, saying," Gofman explained, "is that it was O.K. to go ahead experimenting on humans by allowing exposure [to fallout] so as not to interfere with AEC programs." Gofman has subsequently recommended that scientists like him, who helped to prop up the AEC's bomb testing program, "should be tried before a Nuremberg-type tribunal for crimes against humanity — including human experimentation."

Throughout the government, scientists found that if they produced research results that did not conform with what the AEC wanted them to find, they were in trouble. No one, no matter how highly respected or beyond reproach, was spared the censor's stamp.

In 1971, K. Z. Morgan, after almost 30 years of service at the government's Oak Ridge National Laboratory, learned a hard lesson about the inflexibility of his employers. After several years of research into the possible health hazards of certain plutonium breeder reactors, he was convinced that the technology was not sufficiently safe. He prepared his findings for delivery at an international symposium in Nuremberg. En route, he stopped off in Switzerland for a vacation.

After a week or so, when Morgan was about to board a plane for Nuremberg, he found an urgent message waiting for him. American officials, he was told, were searching frantically for him. Morgan immediately put through a transcontinental call to the deputy director of the

Oak Ridge Lab. The distinguished, world-renowned researcher was informed that his paper, which previously had been approved, was no longer suitable for presentation.

Two hundred copies of the report had been sent ahead to Nuremberg. Incredibly, the Oak Ridge officials asked the West Germans to destroy them. These were replaced, without Morgan's knowledge, with 200 copies of an edited version, with all the critical references to the fast breeder reactor deleted.

By the early 1970s, the nature of the battleground over the hazards of low-level radiation had shifted. Fallout was no longer a political issue, but the burgeoning nuclear power industry was. The Atomic Energy Commission was not only the licensing and regulatory agency concerned with nuclear power plants, but also the government's chief promoter of the new power source. In addition to the formidable resources of the government available to counter nuclear critics, the AEC found welcome allies in the various utility companies across the nation.

Through public lobbying and educational groups such as the Edison Electric Institute and the Atomic Industrial Forum, an intricate network of spokesmen were available to debate nuclear critics and attest to the wonders and safety of atomic power plants. One-time fallout opponents such as Ralph Lapp proved anxious and eager to tout the glories of the nuclear industry. After the horrors of atomic weapons, many physicists were more than ready to help prove that the nuclear genie was worth letting out of the bottle.

One of the first to bear the brunt of the new coalition was Ernest Sternglass. Turning his attention from bomb fallout hazards, the scientist began tilting against the windmills of atomic power in his own backyard — the Shippingport Atomic Power Station, less than 30 miles from his home in Pittsburgh. Using the government's own radiation monitoring reports and vital statistics compiled by the U.S. Public Health Service, Sternglass charged that high levels of radioactive fallout from the Shippingport plant had caused unexplained rises in the infant mortality and cancer rates in the surrounding Beaver Valley.

Pennsylvania Governor Milton Shapp convened a blue-ribbon panel of scientists to investigate Sternglass' alarming charges in 1973. The Atomic Industrial Forum judiciously pulled some of the panel's more critical statements out of context and widely circulated the excerpts as proof that Sternglass had been discredited by his own peers. Yet the scientists didn't disprove the scientist's charges at all. They concluded that "it was impossible to rule out the fact there may have been a relationship between environmental radiation exposure from the Shippingport operations and an increased death rate in the population."

The governor's panel released its report in 1974, noting that the data on monitoring compiled by the government were so poor it was difficult to prove anything decisively one way or another. And the panel still could not account for the fact that the diets of Pittsburgh residents contained abnormally high levels of radiation.

That year in Washington, Dr. Samuel Milham, an epidemiologist with the state department of social and health services, completed his own four-year independent study on the cancer death rates of atomic workers at the government's Hanford plutonium fabrication plant. His work closely paralleled University of Pittsburgh Professor Thomas Mancuso's research project assigned a decade earlier by the AEC.

Milham found that the Hanford workers suffered an increased mortality from cancer of the tongue, mouth and pharynx, colon, pancreas, lung and bone. In May, before publishing his findings, Milham sent a copy of his data to Mancuso for review.

AEC officials were anxious to disprove Milham's contentions. Mancuso came under heavy pressure to publish his own research results prematurely so Milham could be discredited. But the scientist resisted, and sealed his own doom. Within a few days of his refusal to cooperate, the AEC's Dr. James Liverman suddenly decided to terminate the project at Pittsburgh and transfer it to government-controlled facilities. The move was made, it was explained, because of Mancuso's "imminent retirement" — although he was 62 at the time and was allowed to remain at the University of Pittsburgh until age 70.

Mancuso had completed his research by 1976. Not surprisingly, his findings turned out to be the opposite of what the Energy Department, which had by then supplanted the AEC in a cosmetic government reorganization, had hoped for. Instead of disproving Milham, Mancuso agreed with him. The professor had discovered a direct correlation between increased cancer and leukemia rates at doses of radiation below one roentgen.

Dr. Alice Stewart, whose 1958 paper on correlations between in utero radiation exposure and childhood leukemia had been a prime trigger of the low-level radiation controversy, was once again drawn into the fray. Mancuso turned to Stewart for an "independent analysis" of his data. Along with another British scientist, biostatistician George Kneale, Stewart confirmed the validity of Mancuso's findings. John Gofman also conducted an independent analysis of the Hanford workers' death sample compiled by the Pittsburgh professor and confirmed "the association of radiation, accumulated at rates below the permissible rate, with cancer induction."

Mancuso was summarily ordered to turn over his data to scientists at the government-controlled laboratories in Oak Ridge, Tennessee, and the government-contracted Battelle Pacific Northwest Labs in Richland, Washington. None of these scientists had ever conducted a human epidemiological study.

At Battelle, the study was assigned to Dr. Ethel Gilbert, whose preliminary analysis was so abstruse that associates complained they "couldn't make heads or tails of it."

At Oak Ridge, the government hired Dr. Edythalena Tompkins to make an "objective analysis" of the Mancuso data. She had a reputation as an apologist for the nuclear industry. Her husband, Dr. Paul Tompkins, headed the Federal Radiation Council when the permissible levels of iodine in milk was raised secretly. Edythalena Tompkins has proved her allegiance to nuclear interests by commenting publicly that she believed low levels of radiation were not only harmless, but in fact "stimulate the body's natural repair mechanisms."

The government's machinations concerning radiation levels in milk provide a startling example of just how far federal regulators are willing to go to insure the continued development of nuclear power. The utilities themselves are allowed to conduct their own monitoring programs around nuclear power plants. Often, when they find unpleasant evidence, it is suppressed.

For instance, at one dairy farm near the Shippingport, Pennsylvania, plant, Duquesne Light Company–contracted monitors found that the strontium 90 levels in the milk were much higher than federal limits allowed. This particular farm was in the direct path of the prevailing winds that blew from the power plant. The next year, the company simply stopped monitoring at that farm to insure that nothing would be found. By 1979, the government allowed all the utilities to cease monitoring for strontium 90, contending that radioiodine levels in milk would provide adequate warning of dangerous contamination.

The government and the nuclear industry have shown a remarkable ability not only to suppress disagreeable evidence of low-level radiation hazards, but news reports of the cover-up as well. When investigative reporter Jack Anderson unearthed the details of the shady goings-on at Shippingport, the government's quashing of the work of Gofman, Morgan and others, and unreported hazards to nuclear workers and residents living near nuclear power plants, his nationally syndicated column was blacked out in various parts of the country.

Where the column did appear, a flurry of outraged letters to editors also appeared, branding Anderson a liar and calling his allegations "irresponsible." Sometimes the letters were received in newspaper offices days before the offending column was even mailed by Anderson's syndicate. To give the critical barbs a home-town flavor, they were usually signed by a local utility official. Yet when Anderson was able to collect several of the letters from various newspapers across the nation, all of them were identical. Only the signatures changed.

Ralph Lapp publicly branded John Gofman as "beyond the pale of reasonable communication." A top official of the Atomic Industrial Forum once confided to a reporter that the respected scientist had even been committed to a mental hospital — a total fabrication. Sternglass has variously been labeled a crackpot or a fool. Dr. K. Z. Morgan was referred to by his former pupil John Auxier — the AEC technician who was forced to turn back while approaching the Smoky blast — as "irrational." Auxier is today the director of Health Physics at Oak Ridge.

The pattern is obvious. These scientists have been in the forefront, presenting irrefutable evidence that low-level radiation exposure leads to increased cancer and leukemia rates. Since the scientific evidence cannot be disproved, the character and sanity of the scientists are called into question.

A deep schism within the scientific community has developed over the issue of low-level radiation. On one side are government and industry scientists bound and determined not to allow the "nervous Nellies" among their peers to interfere with "progress." They stiffly maintain that the so-called evidence is still lacking. They see the atomic genie as the solution to the energy crunch.

On the other side are America's own dissidents, a group of brave, quixotic characters who have been ostracized and belittled by their own colleagues. Yet the dissidents have of late been joined by a group of unlikely allies: a legion of atomic soldiers — victims of low-level radiation exposure — who by their living and dying serve as the human proof of the low-level radiation-cancer equation.

8

THE BITTER LEGACY

When Russell Jack Dann wheeled through the huge double doors of the House Interstate and Foreign Commerce Committee hearing room on a cold, rainswept morning in January 1978, the first thing he thought was that the place was too damned crowded. He had to crane his neck to peer past the wall of reporters and photographers that surged around his wheelchair.

As he moved down the congested aisle toward the witness table, Dann's eyes surveyed the mahogany-paneled room, taking in the elevated double tier of benches behind which sat the members of Congress, the chairs for a hundred or so spectators with standing room only and, to his right, television cameras nestled on their dollies amid an array of bright lights that burned down from a forest of high metal stands.

Dann wasn't interested in being a showpiece. He just wanted to get his point across and be on his way back home to Albert Lea, Minnesota. After all, nobody had ever believed his story before, except for his wife, Marjorie, and a few former paratroopers like himself, in whom he had confided during some long, wistful nights of story-swapping.

Who would believe that for the sake of a psychological stress test, Russell Dann was marched to a remote desert hilltop and ordered to watch while an atomic device more than three times the size of the bomb dropped on Hiroshima was detonated less than three miles away?

As he waited his turn to go before the microphones, Dann knew that he was the only former enlisted man who had made it to Washington to tell about his experiences during those cool, dawning hours of August 31, 1957, when the detonation of a 48kt device called Smoky helped the sun blast the night into day.

Paul Cooper couldn't come, though without him much of the story of Smoky would remain a mystery. The morning of the hearings, Cooper was lying in a hospital bed near his Elk City, Idaho, home, his body racked with the pain of acute myelogenous leukemia.

Cooper had made the Army a career. Before his 20 years in the service were up in 1972, he had become a Green Beret, pulled two tours of combat in Vietnam and received the Soldier's Medal, the Army's second highest award, for dragging three men from a crashed helicopter in imminent danger of exploding.

After learning that he had leukemia, Cooper told his doctors about witnessing the atomic tests in Nevada. The retired Army sergeant filed a claim for benefits with the Veterans Administration and was denied. Desperate, he told of the agency's hard line in a newspaper story in April 1977.

A week later, the VA belatedly granted Cooper a full disability pension of $820 a month. Though the Veterans Administration Appeals Board finally granted Cooper his due, it never admitted that his leukemia was connected to radiation exposure at Smoky, only that it appeared Cooper had contracted the disease while in the service. Within a month of the Smoky hearings, Cooper would be dead at the age of 44, leaving behind a wife and three children. Immediately after his death, the VA slashed the disability pension benefits to Cooper's family by half.

Cooper had appealed to newspaper and television reporters to tell his story so that "some of my old buddies" who were at the test and who might be in the same shape could help substantiate his claims. Russell Dann had answered the appeal.

Donald Coe didn't make it to testify at the hearings either. He was fogged in at Nashville airport. In 1976 Coe had contacted Congressman Dr. Tim Lee Carter, from his home town of Tompkinsville, Kentucky, about getting the VA to recognize that his chronic back trouble was related to a skiing accident he suffered while stationed in Germany with the Army. The pain, of course, could have been an early sign of leukemia, but Coe's physicians didn't suspect it at the time.

Finally, hairy cell leukemia was diagnosed in December 1976. Coe immediately told his doctors about his presence at atomic tests in the 1950s and filed an initial claim with the VA for service-connected benefits. The agency denied that claim, saying Coe's service records contained no reference to radiation exposure or treatment of radiation sickness.

So it was up to Russell Jack Dann in that hearing room and he was ready. Even the passage of 21 years couldn't dull the vivid recollections the blast of Smoky had etched deeply in his memory. He had come a long way since those days of revelry with Newsome and Hamberger. Dann had neither seen nor heard from his old buddies or Lieutenant Ginn for more than two decades. But he remembered the events of those weeks at Camp Desert Rock as clearly as if they'd occurred only yesterday.

Disillusioned and distraught over what had happened to him at Camp Desert Rock, Dann changed his mind about a career in the Army after his experiences in Nevada. When he got back to Fort Bragg, he was surprised to learn that someone else had been given his job as communications chief.

Within a few days of his return to North Carolina, Dann's company was sent into the field for five days of maneuvers. The corporal had felt sick for days. He was intermittently bothered by nausea and dizzy spells. He could hear only a ringing in one ear. But Dann, disdainful of the fact that "sick call falls to the rear," shrugged off the illness, refusing to visit the base infirmary. The paratroopers jumped from their Hercules C–130 turboprop above a lush green field.

Dann was second man on the stick. He tumbled out the plane's rear door and felt the momentary jerk of the static line automatically pulling his ripcord only seconds after he leaped from the portal. His parachute billowed above him, and then Dann felt the sensation of being snatched back up into the sky as the olive drab canopy filled with air and abruptly slowed his downward plunge.

Caught in a slight crosswind, Dann could see that he was drifting to the right, away from the landing zone and toward a clump of trees. He quickly reached up with his left hand and tugged hard on the parachute riser. The canopy tilted and shifted the direction of the paratrooper's descent back toward the drop zone.

When Dann hit the ground, he scrambled to his feet and gathered in his parachute. But the dizziness wouldn't subside. His head was whirling as he sank to the ground in a heap, retching bilious green liquid. Taking a swig of water from his canteen, Dann gargled and spit the remaining vomit from his mouth. Composing himself, he finished gathering up his parachute and wandered over to where the company commander, Captain Hill, was issuing orders to his men.

The night before the field maneuvers were to end, Dann and another paratrooper were ordered to retrieve the communications wire that had been strung from the unit's "defensive perimeter" through the woods to the company bivouac area. Taking Captain Hill's jeep, they drove to the wire's terminus, only a few hundred yards from the edge of a nearby town. While Dann reeled in the wire, his fellow paratrooper walked into town and bought them a bottle of whiskey.

For three hours they sat in the jeep, merrily quaffing the whiskey. Finally, Dann started the vehicle for the trip back to the bivouac area and promptly backed it into the nearest tree, crushing the rim of the jeep's spare tire and bending the antenna attached to it. Back at camp, Captain Hill was anxiously waiting for Dann's return. The captain wanted to go into town himself. When the two drunken soldiers finally appeared with the smashed jeep, Hill busted Dann in rank right there on the spot.

"Private Dann," the captain glowered at the corporal. "Consider yourself an 'acting jack.' " Though Dann still retained the authority of a corporal and wasn't forced to remove his stripes, he no longer received a corporal's pay.

One of Dann's closest friends in Hill's company had transferred to another training company. Dejected, Dann went to visit him to tell of his latest run-in with their old company commander. He was pleasantly surprised to learn that his friend's company commander was none other than Lieutenant Ginn, Dann's platoon leader at Camp Desert Rock. Dann asked Ginn whether he could transfer to his company, and the lieutenant arranged it.

Newsome also transferred to Ginn's company. He had gotten into a beef with his platoon sergeant. Newsome learned that the sergeant was cheating the soldiers in the company by selling them surplus equipment at inflated prices. When he confronted the man and threatened to tell the rest of the soldiers about the scam, the platoon sergeant promised to make life miserable for Newsome. The sergeant was true to his word, so Newsome left the company for Ginn's unit.

Life in the training company was a pleasant change for Dann and Newsome. Dann became an assistant to the platoon sergeant and prepared lesson plans for new recruits on communications and weaponry. Newsome became the company cook. Both men agreed that the best thing about being in Ginn's company was Ginn.

The lieutenant was both respected and liked by the men under his command. He could always be counted on to back the soldiers up when they were in a fix. Ginn saw to it that Dann was restored to his corporal's rank and even bailed Newsome out of the Fayetteville jail after the fun-loving Virginian had blown the rear wall off a local bar by flushing a powerful artillery simulator down the toilet.

Despite the carefree days spent at the Fort Bragg training command, when Dann's hitch was up in February 1958 he left the Army and took a job selling Singer sewing machines in Charles City, Iowa, ten miles north of his home town of Nashua.

Within a few months, he transferred to the Singer store in Albert Lea, Minnesota, a sleepy town just a few miles north of the Iowa border. Dann didn't prove to be much of a salesman; he simply lacked the will to hawk the sewing machines.

The two major industries of Albert Lea are a Wilson Company beef-packing plant and the Streater Store Fixture Company, which provides cabinets, shelves and decor for thousands of retail businesses across the nation. Since the idea of stuffing intestines with animal viscera didn't appeal to him, Dann got a job as a cabinetmaker at Streater's.

On a blind date a few months later he met a Lake Mills, Iowa, woman named Marjorie Smith who was working as a checkout girl at a local grocery. Her light auburn hair, fresh-scrubbed beauty and unpretentious manner quickly attracted him. In many ways they were very much alike, hot-tempered, yet warm and affectionate. Russell's feistiness was offset by Marjorie's acerbic wit. Her shyness was countered by his outgoing character. After a brief courtship, they married and took an apartment in town.

The dizzy spells that bothered Dann after his return to Fort Bragg continued. Sometimes they were weeks, even months apart, yet they plagued him incessantly. One of the worst spells occurred only weeks after Russell and Marjorie were married.

Driving south toward Lake Mills to visit Marjorie's mother, Dann's head started spinning. He pulled his 1957 Plymouth to the side of the road and asked Marge to take the wheel for the rest of the trip.

On another occasion while in Cedar Rapids, Iowa, installing shelves in a drugstore, Dann plunged from the top of a ladder to the floor during another dizzy spell. He never sought medical help, afraid of what the doctors would find.

In 1960, his hair and teeth began falling out and two years later he discovered that he was sterile. When Dann approached the Veterans Administration with his problem, he was told they had no record that he had ever served in the Army. Disgusted, he let the matter drop.

Dann moved steadily up through the hierarchy at Streater's, ultimately rising to the position as foreman of an installing crew. But the job had its disadvantages. He spent more time on the road than he did in Albert Lea and his marriage suffered under the strain. In 1973, Dann quit Streater's, hoping to salvage what was left of his faltering relationship with Marge. But it was too late. They were divorced that same year.

Anxious to leave the shattered memories of his life with Marjorie behind, Dann began applying for carpentry jobs overseas and on the Alaska pipeline. The dizzy spells were worsening. Dann convinced himself that if he left Albert Lea, all his troubles would also be left behind.

On the night of July 3, 1974, Dann returned to his apartment early in the evening after completing a temporary carpentry job he had taken in town. After a soothing bath, he decided to escape the oppressive heat in his apartment by sleeping on his second-floor balcony. Dann lit up a cigarette and leaned back against the balcony railing as another dizzy spell engulfed him. He blacked out and broke through the rotted wooden railing, falling to the ground below.

Dann regained consciousness several hours later, his body sprawled in a mud puddle. A light rain was pelting him as he tried to get up. He couldn't move his head or legs. Mustering all his bodily strength, Dann somehow managed to drag himself to the side of the building. He screamed and pleaded for help until his voice was hoarse. Picking up a rock, he slammed it repeatedly against the side of the building in a vain attempt to call for help.

Finally, a policeman on routine patrol drove through the alley where Dann lay. After asking the injured man whether he had been drinking, the officer summoned an ambulance. At the local hospital, Dann's attending physician quickly realized that his neck was broken. Better facilities for the treatment of such injuries were available in Minneapolis, and Dann was transferred to a Veterans Administration hospital there within a few hours.

Pneumonia had already set in by the time he reached Minneapolis, 70 miles away. He awoke the next morning in traction, with Marjorie at his side. Once doctors were able to get the pneumonia under control with antibiotics, Dann was transferred once again to the Wood Veterans Hospital in Milwaukee, Wisconsin, where the government maintained a special spinal cord unit dedicated to improving the low survival rate of patients with broken necks.

At Wood, doctors worked desperately to keep Dann alive. Bones from his hip were fused to his shattered spine and a tracheotomy was performed to insure that Dann could continue to breathe even if his severed spinal cord interrupted his brain's automatic signals to his lungs. For eight months he lay in a sophisticated circle bed, his body perfectly motionless and his neck stretched by a series of weights hanging from bolts screwed into his skull.

The dreary months passed painfully. Marjorie often drove to Milwaukee to visit. Dann's truck driver and cabinetmaker friends from Streater's, Gabriel "Gabby" White, Harold "Hody" Hanson and "Big John" Blizek, stopped to see him whenever their delivery routes brought them nearby. But it was hard for them to see their once vibrant, outgoing friend still and mute.

Leona Dann recalled that when Gabby White first saw Russell bolted and strapped in his circle bed, he rushed sobbing from the room and burst into tears. But Leona never gave up hoping, even when Dann's doctors told her there was little chance of her son's survival. When she visited him, she presented a stoic front and shed her tears in the privacy of the austere room at her boardinghouse.

Russell Dann was too ornery to die. After nearly a year in a succession of hospitals, he returned to Albert Lea a wheelchair-bound quadriplegic, determined to pick up the pieces of his broken life. Marjorie nursed and nurtured him, giving him his baths, cooking his meals and dressing him.

Though Dann's legs were useless and his arms and hands twisted and gnarled, his spirit continued to soar. Eighty percent of his voice was lost to the tracheotomy, but Dann still had enough of a croak to mesmerize neighborhood children with tales of past exploits, trade idle threats with his buddies and woo Marjorie once again. They remarried in September 1975 and moved into a ranch-style home with ramps and wide doors to accommodate Dann's wheelchair.

In October 1977 Dann was absent-mindedly watching ABC's "Good Morning America" when he recognized the man host David Hartmann was interviewing. It was Paul Cooper, his fellow squad leader at Camp Desert Rock. Stunned and in a panic, Dann switched the television off with his remote control and wheeled to the phone to call Marge.

"Margie," Dann said excitedly, "it took 20 years but I'm finally right. You hear me, I'm finally right."

"Now settle down, Russell," his wife said in a soothing, but commanding voice. "Settle down and speak slowly. What are you right about?"

"There's a guy on TV named Paul Cooper. He was out at Camp Desert Rock when I was. He claims he's had the same symptoms as me. You know, his hair fell out, dizzy spells. You remember when I applied to the VA for compensation back in the 1960s and they didn't believe me?"

"I remember, Russell," Marjorie said calmly. "Why don't you call this fellow."

"Damn!" Dann abruptly hung up the phone, realizing that he had turned off the television without hearing where Cooper was living. He switched the set back on, but it was too late. The segment of the show with Cooper was over. However, a few days later a newspaper article appeared telling of the retired Army sergeant's plight.

The story mentioned that a Dr. Glyn Caldwell of the government's Center for Disease Control in Atlanta was compiling a list of other soldiers who had been exposed to radiation at Smoky to determine whether they also had suffered similar ailments. Dann called Caldwell and the doctor promised to tell the ailing Cooper that he was trying to reach him.

The newspaper had mentioned that Cooper was an Idaho native and Dann began calling every Cooper in the state trying to locate him. Finally the persistent former paratrooper reached Cooper's brother and learned that his friend was hospitalized in Salt Lake City. Dann rang his room and Cooper's wife, Nancy, answered the telephone. Cooper was gravely ill. The trip to New York for the "Good Morning America" show had been hard on him, but he could chat for a few moments.

The two men talked briefly, reminiscing about the days at Camp Desert Rock. But the small talk drifted quickly to more serious matters.

"Dann, I gotta ask a favor of you," Cooper whispered in a weak, faltering voice.

"Sure, Paul. Anything." Dann responded sprightly.

"If I don't make it," Cooper said ominously, "I want you to follow up on this. They're planning hearings in Washington next year. I'm too sick. If they get hold of you, will you go?"

"Of course I will. But I don't know what to say."

"Just tell the truth."

"O.K., Paul," Dann said, tears welling up in his eyes. "I'll tell it like it was."

Dann listened attentively as Florida Congressman Paul Rogers called his health subcommittee to order and read an opening statement. Then the ranking minority member, Dr. Tim Lee Carter, presented his preliminary statement. They were followed by the first witness, K. Z. Morgan, who put the entire matter into perspective.

"The question before us at this meeting today is not 'Is there a risk of low-level exposure?' or 'What is a safe level of exposure?' Rather it is," Morgan asked earnestly, " 'How great is this risk?' "

Under questioning by the congressmen, Dr. Morgan explained that radiation and its effects were cumulative, even at very low doses. He testified about the deficiencies of the radiation monitoring film badges in use during the atomic tests and confidently stated that "there is no doubt whatsoever" that radiation from the Smoky blast could have caused leukemia among the observers.

The give-and-take between the congressmen and the scientific witnesses lasted well into the afternoon. Though Russell Dann was scheduled to testify that first day, the hearing was adjourned before he was called. He returned to the hearing room the next morning and was immediately called before the microphones.

Dann's throaty voice trembled as he tried to position himself close enough to the microphone to be heard. An aide moved the mike closer to the edge of the table and Dann began reading his statement, slowly and forcefully.

"To all interested personnel. Subject: Atomic bomb test August 31, 1957, called Smoky, Yucca Flat, Nevada. Please note, to the best of my knowledge this résumé contains no secret information, or any top-secret data pertaining to Shot Smoky. Any and all information is to the best of my recollection. Exact yardage, footage, height, location, number of personnel, and magnitude were never clearly explained to our echelon. My explanations are approximate."

Dann coolly related his experiences at Camp Desert Rock and the troubles that had befallen him since. With remarkable accuracy, his testimony was corroborated by official Army reports of the maneuver, with just one major exception. According to the Army after-action reports, all of the troops were removed from the vicinity of the Banded Mountain range. But statements from more than a dozen soldiers and scientists indicate that the HumRRO troops were left behind to bear the brunt of Smoky on Lookout Point.

Dann's presentation was followed by testimony from Colonel Frank Keating, the Task Force Warrior commander who planned the assault by the First Battle Group and helped write the war-game scenario, and Colonel Thomas Stedman, one of the helicopter pilots at Smoky. Both men are retired, pensioned officers.

Keating was anxious to avoid any blame for the sufferings of his men in later years. "It is my opinion," he said adamantly, "that the safeguards and precautions imposed by the Atomic Energy Commission personnel appeared to be adequate to insure safety of all personnel; and to the best of my knowledge none of the individuals who participated in the test from my unit received an overdose of radiation."

Stedman was more circumspect. He pointedly told the committee that he "had two small localized skin cancers removed from my forehead and one from my back. My wife and I have had no children since the atomic tests, and I jokingly said for years that probably I was radioactive from the atomic blast."

Even though much more is known today about the health effects of radiation exposure than in 1957, the AEC's own scientists at the time knew better than to approach ground zero after Smoky. And they were outfitted in protective clothing. Why, then, were the soldiers permitted to maneuver through the highly contaminated areas? The Army's own reports revealed that the major purpose of the exercise was public relations. Yet those reports also noted that all planned Army maneuvers had to be cleared a week in advance with the AEC director at Camp Mercury. The answer to the key question will probably never be fully known.

Dosimetry and radiation badges at Smoky were crude at best. The readings recorded by many film badges taken from soldiers who had traversed the contaminated area were inexplicably low. Russell Dann's film badge, for example, recorded a gamma dose of only 2.24 roentgens, less than half the permissible exposure. Yet Major Alan Skerker, who was assigned to review the Army's records on atmospheric bomb testing, admitted that at the time of Smoky, Army records showed that "no available rate meter meets military specifications and measures beta radiation satisfactorily. Casualties could easily result from beta burns received in a contaminated area indicated safe by gamma instruments.''

Not only were radiation film badges at Smoky incapable of monitoring beta doses or the plutonium-bred alpha emitters from the bomb, but thousands of radiation exposure records are missing. Some undoubtedly were lost during a fire at a federal records storage center in St. Louis in 1976, but others simply disappeared. Gary Hamberger, for instance, still has the film badge he wore in 1957. How many other soldiers at the blasts never bothered to turn their film badges in? The question will go unanswered because information on the film badges is unavailable.

Robert Kingsbury was a young Army captain when he watched the detonation of Shot Kepler during the Plumbbob series. The wind shifted at the last moment and dumped a cloud of fallout on Kingsbury and the other observers in the trenches. The contamination was duly noted in his permanent Army medical record at the time.

Kingsbury saw the notation at least 15 times before his records were lost while he was stationed in the Dominican Republic in 1965. He tried unsuccessfully to locate a duplicate copy of his medical records both before and after he retired from the Army after 23 years in 1969. The former Army major finally got a copy of the missing file ten years later, and though the document included his medical history all the way back to World War II, the one page containing the medical notation of radiation exposure was mysteriously absent.

Kingsbury, now the director of the Los Angeles County Department of Military and Veterans' Affairs, is plagued with skin cancer. However, Kingsbury, like Russell Dann, has no unkind words for the Army both men love. He simply wonders why there were never follow-up checks on the men who were exposed to radiation.

Others are not so forgiving. Official records show Donald Coe had nosebleeds and other signs of radiation sickness while he was still at Camp Desert Rock. Paul Cooper showed leukemia symptoms as early as 1968, four years before he retired from the Army.

Cooper's widow, Nancy, softly lamented, ''They were promised checkups. If they had looked they would have found that Paul had leukemia when it was still in its chronic stage. They just never followed up on these thousands and thousands of men, and now they are dying. I feel it's just the same as if they'd shot him. They took his life.''

Physician-Congressman Tim Lee Carter championed the Smoky veterans' cause after his constituent Donald Coe first came to him for help. True to his Hippocratic oath to relieve human suffering, the gentle, ambling country doctor was a driving force behind the committee's probe of the health effects of low-level radiation.

Tossing aside any notion of partisan politics, Carter and Chairman Rogers called dozens of Pentagon and Energy Department officials on the congressional carpet. They assailed the generals, admirals and bureaucrats with pointed questions about the disappearance of medical records, the laxity of radiation safety and the suppression of scientific research linking low-level radiation, in amounts previously thought harmless, to increased incidence of leukemia and cancer. Unfortunately, both congressmen later retired.

Before they left the House, the two congressmen also joined forces to protect the integrity of an epidemiological study of the Smoky soldiers conducted by the Center for Disease Control. Carter and Rogers successfully blocked attempts by the Pentagon and the Energy Department to gain control of the CDC study in 1979. After all, it had been a former CDC physician who recognized that Cooper's illness might have been just one of many afflictions produced by the bomb blasts.

The whole puzzle began to unravel in late November 1976, when an epidemiologist at the Veterans Administration Hospital in Salt Lake City learned of Cooper's case and alerted his former colleagues in Atlanta. After painstaking, methodical research combing Army files and death certificates, Dr. Glyn Caldwell has managed to compile a list of 3,224 men who were present at Shot Smoky. Among them Caldwell identified eight confirmed cases of leukemia.

"We managed to find birth dates for 2,887 of the men. Only 1,988 corresponded with us," Caldwell explained. "But we have data on 12 more which gives us a total of 2,000 men we've located completely."

"Now, using the number 2,887, for which we have birth dates," Caldwell continued, "we would expect to find 101 cancers, including leukemias. At last count our total cancers were 111. Now the only real increase in the number of those cancers that has any statistical significance is the leukemias. Among all of the men who were there — 3,224 — we would expect to find that about 3.5 had leukemia. We've already found 8 among 2,887. That's a doubling of the expected incidence."

Incredibly, most of the leukemia victims received doses of radiation, according to their film badges, below 3 roentgens. One was as low as 1.25r. "Now, the cases of leukemia among the Smoky men could be unique," Caldwell suggested. "But I doubt it. All of these things indicate that something is going on that we don't quite understand. The best data available is the Japanese studies of A-bomb survivors. There's no argument that radiation increases cancer risk. The question is how little radiation does it take to increase the risk and whether the curve is a straight line down to zero or curvilinear. The big problem is, will anyone believe us when we're done."

Many cancers induced by radiation remain latent for years. They only show up decades later after festering and growing, hidden among the body's cells. Cancers that may have been triggered by fallout or other radiation decades ago are beginning to appear after years of dormancy.

According to a 1978 study of Hiroshima and Nagasaki A-bomb survivors conducted by Drs. Gilbert Beebe, Hiroo Kato and Charles Land of the Radiation Effects Research Foundation, "in addition to leukemia and cancer of thyroid, breast, and lung, now cancer of the esophagus, stomach, and urinary organs, and the lymphomas, should be included among the forms of cancer caused by the ionizing radiation from the 1945 atomic explosions."

"We haven't yet found an increase in lymphomas among the Smoky soldiers," said Caldwell, "but that doesn't mean it won't show up. There are lymphomas among them, but not in excess."

Excesses in leukemia have proved abundant, and not just among the soldiers exposed to radiation at the atomic blasts. As Linus Pauling predicted decades ago, the children have suffered along with the soldiers.

According to a 1979 paper published in the *New England Journal of Medicine* by Drs. Joseph Lyon, Melville Klauber, John Gardner and King Udall, the leukemia mortality rate among children below age 15 exposed to large amounts of fallout in Utah "increased by 2.44 times . . . and was greatest in 10-to-14-year-old children." The findings only confirm the doubling in leukemia rates found among the Smoky veterans. The striking leukemia death toll among the 3,224 veterans of Smoky may be only the beginning.

The Pentagon estimates that between 250,000 and 500,000 American soldiers, airmen, sailors, Marines and civilians were exposed to radiation during 184 atmospheric nuclear bomb tests between 1946 and the atmospheric test ban treaty of 1963. Ninety-eight of them were exploded in the South Pacific, and eighty-six at the Nevada Test Site.

The Defense Nuclear Agency set up a toll-free telephone hot line with operators on duty 24 hours a day, seven days a week to receive calls from veterans of the nuclear blasts. But the Pentagon's attempts to locate the veterans, or to publicize the existence of the hot line, have been only halfhearted. Instead, the Defense Department's efforts have been directed at writing long-winded, detailed reports on each of the bomb blasts and trying to reevaluate the true doses of radiation the soldiers might have received. Officials say that 99 percent of those exposed to the bombs received a dose of less than one roentgen.

Meanwhile, new atomic soldiers are being exposed to radiation every day. With a $20 million appropriation from Congress, the Defense Nuclear Agency is directing cleanup operations on Eniwetok atoll. The soldiers, sailors and airmen involved in the operation wear special protective clothing, and, according to the Pentagon, their radiation doses are "limited to the lowest levels practicable."

Using bulldozers, backhoes and other earth-moving equipment, the cleanup portion of the program consists of three separate efforts: removal and lagoon-dumping of uncontaminated debris and structures, removal and crater entombment of radiologically contaminated debris, and excision and crater entombment of some of the radiologically contaminated soil that remains on the islands.

The contaminated material is moved to Runit Island and placed in one of two concrete-lined craters created by previous explosions. When the craters are filled, they will be capped with concrete and the island will be declared in quarantine forever.

Similar previous attempts by the government to clean up its nuclear garbage and make contaminated islands inhabitable once again have failed miserably. More than a decade ago the U.S. agreed to let 500 Bikinians return to their contaminated island after it was ostensibly safe. An AEC spokesman confidently declared that there was "virtually no radiation left." But in March 1978 government scientists discovered that they had blundered badly. The water on the island still contained harmful amounts of fallout and so did the coconuts, fruits and vegetables grown there. The islanders were forced to evacuate once again.

For the thousands of American soldiers exposed to radiation during bomb tests, there can be no evacuation and no escape from the effects of the shots. For them, there is only an ongoing battle with the bureaucratic red tape that snarls their attempts to win compensation.

EPILOGUE

ALBERT LEA, MINNESOTA
JANUARY 1980

When a nation calls upon its youth to sacrifice their bodies and their lives for an ideal, there remains a moral obligation to the warriors and their families long after the battles have been fought and won. After the Civil War, Abraham Lincoln was quick to recognize that obligation and act on it. "We must care for those who have borne the battle," he declared compassionately, "and for their widows and orphans."

Though Lincoln's timeless admonition is etched deeply into the granite of the Veterans Administration headquarters building in downtown Washington, those who bore the brunt of the atomic battles of the cold war have been rebuffed time and time again in their attempts to obtain government compensation for what they claim are radiation-related illnesses.

In spite of the overwhelming mass of evidence to the contrary and the accusing stare of history, the government refuses to admit any correlation between the maladies of the atomic soldiers and their exposure to radiation at bomb tests in Nevada and the South Pacific.

To add insult to injury, a federal court decision known as the Feres Doctrine prohibits servicemen or their survivors from suing the government on grounds of negligence for injuries sustained while in the Armed Forces. Soldiers also are limited to spending $10 in legal fees for the preparation of their claims to the Veterans Administration. The agency is the final arbiter of those claims; decisions by the Veterans Administration cannot be appealed in civil court.

Thousands of veterans of the blasts are reported to be suffering from a variety of cancers. But beyond the visible effects of radiation exposure, there is a real concern among the atomic soldiers that it is their offspring who will become the walking wounded, saddled with the legacy of the atomic age for generations to come. Already many of the veterans have reported an extraordinary number of genetic deformities among their children. The atomic soldiers must also deal with myriad psychological and emotional illnesses bred by their experience — and guilt.

Russell Jack Dann returned to the Wood Veterans Hospital for a routine checkup only days after his testimony at the Smoky hearings. The doctors found that he had yet another ailment to contend with — leukopenia — a low white blood cell count that may, or may not, be a precursor to leukemia. Dann has applied to the VA for compensation four times. His claims have been consistently denied.

The trials and tribulations of the last few years of Dann's life have only strengthened his resolve. His adjustment to existence in a wheelchair amazes his friends. They can still detect the spark of mischievousness in his eyes, the bluster of his youth and the familiar cockiness of a bantam rooster.

It's almost possible to tell the days of the week by keeping track of the visitors to the Dann's suburban Albert Lea home. On Mondays, Elwood "Red" Jensen often stops by to chew the fat. Jensen owns a local towing service, Tow 'n' Travel, and has made Dann the company dispatcher. An easygoing, friendly man with a wild shock of bright red hair, Jensen is never too busy to take a break from his work to make minor adjustments to the specially equipped van that enables the quadriplegic to drive while seated in his wheelchair. Jensen also provides his dispatcher with free gas and oil.

On Tuesdays, Big John Blizek usually stops by for a visit. A cabinet-maker at Streater's, Blizek's gentle manner belies his bearlike size. Kneeling in a corner, he often makes plans with Dann for a weekend outing while softly stroking the family's dog, Tiger. A friend since Dann's days as a cabinetmaker, the shy, soft-spoken Blizek laughs heartily at Russell's jokes and fills him in on the latest goings-on at Streater's.

At midweek, Marjorie's boss, Jim Bergstrom, can always be counted on to enliven the atmosphere with humorous tales of his Scandinavian family's exploits during the wild and woolly days of Minnesota life at the beginning of the century. He is the proprietor of a thriving plumbing business and is always eager to garner a laugh at the expense of fellow practitioners of his art. Marjorie serves as the bookkeeper of his business and attests to the accuracy of Bergstrom's tongue-in-cheek descriptions of the plumbing profession.

On Thursdays and Fridays Streater truck drivers roll into town after their cross-country delivery trips. A frequent and welcome visitor to the Danns' home is Gabby White. Mustachioed and clad in cowboy boots, White spends most of his time good-naturedly harassing Dann — and vice versa. The two men served in the Minnesota National Guard until Dann's accident, and their repartee is reminiscent of the boisterous give-and-take of the barracks.

Truck driver Hody Hanson also visits regularly at the end of every week. Over a can of beer, Hanson and Dann talk of the carefree days they spent in the early 1960s, riding across the countryside on their Harley-Davidson motorcycles.

The attention of his friends keeps Dann's spirits up and the part-time job as a tow-truck dispatcher helps him pass the monotonous days at home. One corner of the family recreation room is cluttered with an array of short-wave and citizens band radios, microphones, tape recorders, books about atomic testing, a typewriter and memorabilia of the 82nd Airborne Division all resting upon shelves and workbenches attached to the wall at a height that allows Dann to reach everything from his wheelchair.

His chair is brightly festooned with bumper stickers; a pair of para-trooper's jump wings is pinned to the back. To prevent sores from developing, Dann often raises his body from the chair by pushing down on the armrests with his forearms. Though the activity leaves bloody, scab-covered wounds on his elbows, Dann seems oblivious to them.

Says Marjorie, ''Russell's still as feisty as he always was, but I guess these days he's even spoiled worse than ever.''

Dann reacts to his wife's jesting criticism with a chuckle and a look of mock innocence. ''Margie,'' he says, ''has got my number. You betcha she does.''

Dann's personal quest to track down the members of his Camp Desert Rock platoon seems to have given him a new purpose. Information he may obtain that would help his claims before the Veterans Administration is incidental. All Dann really wants to do is find his former Army buddies and talk about old times. His days in the Army are remembered fondly. After all, then he was Corporal Russell Jack Dann, a perfect physical specimen with two good legs and two strong arms. The memories linger, and when the voice of an old acquaintance like Newsome crackles over the phone, Dann's face lights up with a smile.

Like hundreds of other veterans of atomic blasts, Dann says he would do it all again, even knowing what he knows today. The monetary payments he would be entitled to if his claim was approved by the Veterans Administration mean nothing to him. "All I want," Dann insists, "is for the government to tell the truth. To admit that they sent us to watch that bomb and recognize that because we were ordered onto Yucca Flat, we have suffered. If I had broken my leg on maneuvers or gotten shot, I'd have been compensated. Well, I was shot by radiation, and the Army should own up to it."

Chuck Newsome returned to his home town of Hampton, Virginia, when he left the Army soon after Dann. He spent several years as a manager of a professional hockey team and then started his own sign-painting business. Though the years have taken their toll on Newsome, they have changed him little. He remains the gregarious, fun-loving Virginian, always ready for an adventure.

Today Newsome is 43 years old and bothered by arthritis and neck and chest pain. He has had prostrate trouble since he left the service in his early twenties. The father of three sons and a daughter, Newsome lives with his wife, Linda, on a 52-foot houseboat in Hampton Harbor.

Gary Hamberger returned to his own company at Fort Bragg after the trip to Nevada. Occasionally he would spot Newsome and Dann on the sprawling Army base, but the three men drifted apart. Hamberger left the Army in 1958 and returned to York, Pennsylvania, where after a few months he landed a job with the local water company. Four years later, he became a truck driver for the United Parcel Service and began working his way up the company hierarchy.

Today Hamberger is the supervisor of UPS operations in York and lives with his wife, Paula, and their four children in a rambling white house that once served as the administrative building for the local airport. His health is excellent, and Hamberger still has the solid, taut look of his youth. One thing has changed: he doesn't always win at craps anymore.

Sergeant David Icenhour retired from the Army on a medical disability in 1971 and settled in North Carolina. At the age of 47, he suffers from heart disease and thyroid problems.

Private Robert Schaudenecker returned to his home town of Chicago after his hitch in the Army and resumed his career as a firefighter. Today he is a captain on the force and, according to his doctors, suffers from a low white blood cell count similar to Russell Dann's.

Lieutenant William Crites, a Task Force Big Bang platoon leader, remained in the Army, ultimately rising to the rank of colonel and serving as the administrator of the Walter Reed Army Hospital. His health is excellent.

Lieutenant Ginn, Dann's platoon leader, left active duty in 1960 and settled in Richmond, Virginia, with his wife and two children. The enterprising former Army officer spent several years as an industrial engineer and then went into business with a friend. Ginn is now a brigadier general in the Army Reserve, sits on the board of directors of a local bank and is co-owner of a thriving lighting-store chain. Like Crites, his health is also excellent.

"We never really thought any of our troops would have any problems with radiation," Ginn said recently, adding with a laugh, "we expected most of them would end up with venereal disease, they spent so much time in Beatty."

Captain Stovall and Douglas the bugler seem to have disappeared without a trace. Attempts by Dann and others to find them, or even to determine whether they are dead or alive, have failed.

Twenty years after the Plumbbob series, Ann Mark, the AEC clerk-typist who watched all of the bomb blasts from 30 miles away, contracted cervical cancer. Her doctors won't rule out the possibility that the disease could have been induced by radiation exposure. Mark has sued the government for six million dollars, charging that her injuries were sustained because of negligence by the AEC.

Donald Coe, a private with the First Battle Group at Smoky, did receive a disability pension from the VA after the Smoky hearings, but, as usual, the agency refused to recognize any connection between his illness and radiation exposure.

Among the monkeys exposed at the Smoky test, the leukemia death rate two decades later was more than twice the average incidence.

None of the researchers who made up the HumRRO psychological research team at Smoky are still with the organization. But HumRRO is still going strong. Now a private, nonprofit consulting firm headquartered in Alexandria, Virginia, the Pentagon is still the organization's prime source of contract work.

Orville Kelly, the Army sergeant in the charge of Japtan Island during Operation Hardtack, was told by his doctors in 1974 that he had lymphocytic lymphoma (cancer of the lymph nodes) in an advanced stage. The founder of a self-help organization for terminal cancer patients called Make Today Count, Kelly is also the prime force behind the National Association of Atomic Veterans, an information clearinghouse on the atomic tests that is run from his Burlington, Iowa, home. With his wife, Wanda, Kelly publishes a monthly newsletter and offers advice to fellow atomic soldiers on obtaining Army records. Finally, Kelly's claim to the VA for service-connected benefits was granted, but as in all previous cases, the government admitted no connection between his disease and radiation exposure.

Harry Coppola, the Marine sent to Nagasaki to keep order after the A-bomb was dropped, fell from a ladder while working as a painter in 1974 and broke several ribs. The ribs would not heal, and after a bone marrow test, his doctors found high levels of radiation in his body and diagnosed his problem as multiple myeloma — a rare form of bone marrow cancer.

At least 40 others among the first thousand or so Americans to approach the bombed-out city of Nagasaki have also contracted multiple myeloma, leukemia or blood disorders. The high incidence of the diseases among so few men is startling. Repeated attempts by Coppola and other veterans of the Nagasaki cleanup to gain compensation from the government have all failed.

Over the past decade, some 400 veterans have filed claims with the Veterans Administration for radiation-related injuries. Fewer than two dozen have been approved, and in none of the cases have ailments based solely on radiation exposure been enough to win compensation.

The government is taking a cautious line. Pentagon officials claim that 99 percent of the servicemen exposed to radiation during the atmospheric tests received a smaller dose than prudence allowed.

The government has eagerly compensated Marshall Islanders for radiation injuries they sustained, either real or imagined, at a rate of $25,000 for every man, woman, and child. However, there are only a few hundred of the islanders. The atomic soldiers number in the hundreds of thousands.

Any admission that radiation exposure at the low levels received by the atomic soldiers can be linked to increased incidence of leukemia and cancer could prove devastating. It is not the few million dollars that might have to be paid to veterans that has the bureaucrats in Washington on edge. Rather, it is the fear that the admission of a causal relationship between low-level radiation and cancer might open up the government and the nuclear industry to a host of lawsuits by current and former nuclear workers and fallout victims exposed to radiation levels that have always been considered safe.

Already attorneys representing hundreds of cancer victims or their survivors have filed suit in federal court charging that nuclear fallout led to their diseases and deaths. Most of the claimants lived in Utah, Nevada and Arizona communities downwind from the Nevada Test Site during the atmospheric detonations. They are seeking hundreds of millions of dollars in compensation, charging that the government "failed to use reasonable care to conduct a safe nuclear experimentation program at the test site."

It's not likely that the government will reverse long-standing policies or repudiate the actions of 35 years. So while the latest in a long line of politicians posture and profess their concern, Russell Dann and thousands like him wait. There will be calls for more research and more proof.

The atomic soldiers end up caught in a deadly race between the diseases that engulf their bodies and the ever-ponderous government. It is a contest that the soldiers are losing, and they are paying the price of defeat, as warriors always do, with their lives.

DOCUMENTARY REFERENCES

Prologue
Armed Forces Talk, U.S. Department of Defense, September 19, 1952.

Chapter 1
"Report Covering the Selection of Proposed Emergency Proving Ground for the United States Atomic Energy Commission," by the engineering firm of Holmes and Narver, August 14, 1950.

"Discussion of Radiological Hazards Associated with a Continental Test Site for Atomic Bombs," minutes of a meeting held at the Los Alamos Scientific Laboratory, Los Alamos, New Mexico, August 1, 1950.

Memorandum for the Special Committee of the National Security Council for Atomic Energy Matters from AEC Chairman Gordon Dean, December 13, 1950.

Memorandum for the Secretary of State, the Secretary of Defense and the Chairman, Atomic Energy Commission from James S. Lay, Executive Secretary, National Security Council, December 14, 1950.

"Selection of a Continental Test Site," by Colonel K. E. Fields, Director, AEC Division of Military Application, December 1950.

Atomic Energy Commission Meeting No. 515, January 10, 1951.

"Operation Ranger: Operational Program Reports," by the Los Alamos Scientific Laboratory, University of California, Vol. V, January-February 1951.

Atomic Energy Commission Meeting No. 541, March 26, 1951.

Atomic Energy Commission Meeting No. 549, April 17, 1951.

Atomic Energy Commission Meeting No. 551, April 25, 1951.

Atomic Energy Commission Meeting, No. 573, June 27, 1951.

Memorandum for Gordon Dean, Chairman of the Atomic Energy Commission from Colonel H. McK. Roper, Executive Secretary, AEC Military Liaison Committee, July 16, 1951.

Memorandum for the Chairman, Military Liaison Committee from AEC Chairman Gordon Dean, August 3, 1951.

Memorandum for Carroll Tyler, Manager, Santa Fe Operations Office from M. W. Boyer, General Manager, AEC Test Site, September 20, 1951.

Chapter 2

Memorandum for Carroll Tyler, Manager, Santa Fe Operations Office from Shields Warren, M.D., Director, AEC Division of Biology and Medicine, October 11, 1951.

"A Study of Soldier Attitudes and Knowledge about Atomic Effects: Exercise Desert Rock I," compiled jointly by the Attitude Research Branch, Department of Defense and the Attitude Assessment Branch, Department of the Army, October-November 1951.

"Desert Rock I: A Psychological Study of Troop Reactions to an Atomic Explosion," by Peter A. Bordes, John L. Finan, Joseph R. Hochstim, Howard H. McFann, and Shepard G. Schwartz, Human Resources Research Office Technical Report No. 1, February 1953. AD–6092.

"Troop Performance on a Training Maneuver Involving the Use of Atomic Weapons," by Alfred H. Hausrath, Suzanne G. Billingsley, Stanley W. Davis, Henry P. Griggs, and Florence Trefethen; in collaboration with Lewis M. Killian, John D. Montgomery, Harley O. Preston, and Paul V. Trovillo; and assisted by Nathaniel R. Kidder, Mary G. Page, Gladys E. Post, and Shirley C. Dunn, Operations Research Office, The Johns Hopkins University, March 15, 1952.

Memorandum for Colonel K. E. Fields, AEC Director of Military Application from Brigadier General Herbert Loper, Chief, Armed Forces Special Weapons Project, November 26, 1951.

Letter from Colonel K. E. Fields, AEC Director of Military Application to Brigadier General Herbert Loper, Chief, Armed Forces Special Weapons Project, December 28, 1951.

Memorandum for the Chief, Armed Forces Special Weapons Project from General J. Lawton Collins, Chief of Staff, U.S. Army; General Hoyt S. Vandenberg, Chief of Staff, U.S. Air Force; and Admiral W. M. Fechteler, Chief of Naval Operations, January 18, 1952.

Letter from Brigadier General A. R. Luedecke, Deputy Chief, Armed Forces Special Weapons Project to Colonel K. E. Fields, Director, AEC Division of Military Application, March 7, 1952.

Memorandum for Brigadier General K. E. Fields, Director, AEC Division of Military Application from Shields Warren, M.D., Director, AEC Division of Biology and Medicine, March 25, 1952.

Atomic Energy Commission Meeting No. 677, April 1, 1952.

Letter from AEC Chairman Gordon Dean to Brigadier General Herbert Loper, Chief, Armed Forces Special Weapons Project, April 2, 1952.

"Troop Participation in Operation Tumbler-Snapper," report of the Director, AEC Division of Military Application, March 1952.

"Desert Rock IV: Reactions of an Armored Infantry Battalion to an Atomic Bomb Maneuver," Human Resources Research Office Technical Report No. 2, August 1953. AD–16451.

"Reactions of Troops in Atomic Maneuvers: Exercise Desert Rock IV," by Suzanne G. Billingsley, John C. Balloch, and Alfred H. Hausrath, Operations Research Office, The Johns Hopkins University, July 15, 1953.

"Gain in Information in the Desert Rock A-Bomb Maneuvers," by Berton Winograd, Human Resources Research Office Staff Memorandum, March 1954. AD–482 184.

Atomic Energy Commission Meeting No. 688, May 2, 1952.

Minutes of the meeting of the Advisory Committee for Biology and Medicine held in St. Louis, Missouri, June 7–9, 1952.

Memorandum for John Bugher, M.D., Director, AEC Division of Biology and Medicine from Captain John T. Hayward, Chief, Navy Weapons Research Branch, September 19, 1952.

Letter to Carroll Tyler, Manager, AEC Santa Fe Operations Office from Colonel Paul Preuss, Director, Weapons Effects Tests, Armed Forces Special Weapons Project, September 22, 1952. Subject: Troop radiation exposure limits.

Memorandum for Brigadier General K. E. Fields, Director, AEC Division of Military Application from George P. Kraker, Deputy Manager, AEC Santa Fe Operations Office, October 7, 1952. Subject: Reply to Captain Hayward regarding troop participation in atomic tests.

Letter to Brigadier General K. E. Fields, Director, AEC Division of Military Application from Major General Herbert Loper, Chief, Armed Forces Special Weapons Project, October 15, 1952.

"Troop Participation in Continental Tests," report by the Director, AEC Division of Military Application, December 1952.

Atomic Energy Commission Meeting No. 794, December 23, 1952.

Chapter 3

Letter to Major General Herbert Loper, Chief, Armed Forces Special Weapons Project from M. W. Boyer, General Manager, AEC Test Site, January 8, 1953.

"Exercise Desert Rock V: Operation Reports," by the staff of Headquarters, U.S. Sixth Army, January–June 1953.

Memorandum for the Assistant Chief of Staff, U.S. Army G-3 from Colonel H. C. Donnelly, Acting Chief, Armed Forces Special Weapons Project. Subject: Troop participation in Exercise Desert Rock V. January 26, 1953. Attachments from Commandant, U.S. Marine Corps; Chief of Naval Operations; and Chief, U.S. Navy Bureau of Medicine and Surgery.

Memorandum for the Record, U.S. Army G-3. Subject: Troop radiation dose exposure limits for Exercise Desert Rock V. February 24, 1953.

Letter to AEC Chairman Gordon Dean from Major General F. L. Parks, U.S. Army Chief of Information. Subject: Army responsibility for the safety of news correspondents. February 27, 1953.

Letter to President Dwight D. Eisenhower from Helen M. Dodds, March 15, 1953.

Letter to Helen Dodds from Colonel H. C. Donnelly, Acting Chief of Staff, Armed Forces Special Weapons Project, April 29, 1953.

"Report of Participation in Selected Volunteer Program of Desert Rock V-7," by Captain Robert A. Hinners, USN, Armed Forces Special Weapons Project, April 25, 1953.

"Desert Rock V: Reactions of Troop Participants and Forward Volunteer Officer Groups to Atomic Exercises," by Benjamin W. White, Human Resources Research Office Information Report, August 1953. AD–478 053.

"Operation Upshot-Knothole Project 8.5: Thermal Radiation Protection Afforded Test Animals by Fabric Assemblies," by the staff of the Headquarters Field Command, Armed Forces Special Weapons Project, Sandia Base, Albuquerque, New Mexico, March–June 1953.

Atomic Energy Commission Meeting No. 862, May 13, 1953.

Atomic Energy Commission Meeting No. 863, May 18, 1953.

Atomic Energy Commission Meeting No. 865, May 21, 1953.

Atomic Energy Commission Meeting No. 866, May 22, 1953.

Diary of AEC Chairman Gordon Dean, May 22–27, 1953.

Meeting of Livestockmen and AEC officials, Cedar City, Utah, January 13, 1954.

Atomic Energy Commission Meeting No. 884, July 7, 1953.

Atomic Energy Commission Meeting No. 1032, October 5, 1954.

"Exercise Desert Rock VI: Final Report of Operations," by the staff of Headquarters, U.S. Sixth Army, August 1955.

"Report of Exercise Desert Rock VI: Marine Corps," compiled by the Third Marine Corps Provisional Atomic Exercise Brigade Staff, March 1955.

Atomic Energy Commission Meeting No. 1062, February 23, 1955.

Chapter 4

"Plumbbob Off-Site Rad-Safety Report: Off-Site Radiological Safety Activities of the Nevada Test Organization," United States Atomic Energy Commission, September 1958.

"Atomic Tests in Nevada," United States Atomic Energy Commission, March 1957.

"Continental Atomic Tests: Background Information for Observers," United States Atomic Energy Commission, August 1957.

"Operation Plumbbob: On-Site Radiological Safety Support Report," compiled and edited by members of the Reynolds Electrical and Engineering Company, Inc., Radiological Safety Division, United States Atomic Energy Commission, September 1957.

Chapter 5
"Experiences at Desert Rock VIII," by Robert D. Baldwin, Human Resources Research Office Staff Memorandum, March 1958.

Chapter 6
"Exercise Desert Rock VII and VIII: Final Report of Operations," by the staff of Headquarters, U.S. Sixth Army, November 1957.

"Infantry Troop Exercise: Exercise Desert Rock VII and VIII," by the staff of Headquarters, U.S. Sixth Army, August 1957.

"Report of Test Infantry Troop Test: Exercise Desert Rock VII and VIII," by the staff of Headquarters, U.S. Sixth Army, January 22, 1958.

Chapter 7
"Operation Hardtack — Phase II: Off-Site Radiological Safety Report, Off-Site Radiological Safety Activities," United States Atomic Energy Commission Technical Information Service, 1958.

"Fallout, Radiation Standards, and Countermeasures," hearings before the Joint Committee on Atomic Energy, June 2, 4, and 6, 1963.

"Fallout, Radiation Standards, and Countermeasures," hearings before the Joint Committee on Atomic Energy, August 20, 21, 22, and 27, 1963.

"Shippingport Nuclear Power Station: Alleged Health Effects," report to the Governor of Pennsylvania, 1974.

"Annual Environmental Report: Beaver Valley Power Station and Shippingport Atomic Power Station — 1975," by the Duquesne Light Company.

"Annual Environmental Report: Beaver Valley Power Station and Shippingport Atomic Power Station — 1976," by the Duquesne Light Company.

Chapter 8
"Effect of Radiation on Human Health," hearings before the Subcommittee on Health and the Environment of the Committee on Interstate and Foreign Commerce, U.S. House of Representatives, January 24–26, February 8, 9, 14, and 28, 1978.

"Leukemia among Persons Present at an Atmospheric Nuclear Test (Smoky)," *Morbidity and Mortality Weekly Report*, U.S. Department of Health, Education, and Welfare, Center for Disease Control, August 10, 1979.

Gilbert W. Beebe, Hiroo Kato, and Charles E. Land, "Studies of the Mortality of A-Bomb Survivors," *Radiation Research* 75, 1978, pp. 138–201.

Joseph L. Lyon, M.D., M.P.H.; Melville R. Klauber, Ph.D.; John W. Gardner, M.D.; and King S. Udall, M.D.; "Childhood Leukemias Associated with Fallout from Nuclear Testing," *New England Journal of Medicine*, February 22, 1979, pp. 397–402.

"Analysis of Radiation Exposure for Task Force Warrior Shot Smoky: Exercise Desert Rock VII–VIII, Operation Plumbbob," by Science Applications, Inc., May 31, 1979.

Epilogue

Feres v. *United States*, 340 US Code 135, 95 L ed 152, 71 S Ct 153.

Additional References

"Announced United States Nuclear Test Statistics," compiled by the Office of Public Affairs, U.S. Department of Energy, Nevada Operations Office, Las Vegas, December 1978.

The Effects of Nuclear Weapons, compiled and edited by Samuel Glasstone and Philip J. Dolan, 3rd edition prepared and published by the United States Department of Defense and the United States Department of Energy, 1977.

"Public Safety and Underground Nuclear Detonations," United States Atomic Energy Commission, Division of Technical Information Extension, Oak Ridge, Tennessee, June 1971.

"Radiation Standards and Public Health: Proceedings of a Second Congressional Seminar on Low-Level Ionizing Radiation," sponsored by the Congressional Environmental Study Conference, the Environmental Policy Institute and the Atomic Industrial Forum, February 10, 1978.

INDEX

A

A is for Atom (film), 77
Abelson, Dr. Philip, 139-140
Adams, Sherman, 59
AEC, *see* Atomic Energy Commission
Alamogordo-White Sands Guided Missile Range, 30
American Association for the Advancement of Science, 147-148
American Medical Association, 144
Anderson, Sen. Clint, 71-73
Anderson, Jack, 153
Annie shot, 59
Argonne National Laboratory, 137
Armed Forces Special Weapons Project, 25, 48, 56
Atomic bomb: creation of, 21-22; dropped on Japan, 22-24; programs for peaceful use of, 136-137, 139-140, 147
Atom-bomb testing program, U.S.: AEC's report on possible continental test sites, 29-30; Defense Department figures on, 167; meeting for discussion of possible continental, 26-29. *See also specific test site locations*
Atomic Energy (film), 77
Atomic Energy Commission: beginning problems with radioactive fallout, 63-68; controversy with Defense Department over soldier participation in blasts, 42-43, 48-55, 56-57; and development of Nevada Test Site, 31-35, 36-39; effect of fallout patterns on shot schedules of, 70-74; establishment of, 24-25; and H-bomb debate, 25-26; influence of information published in *Science* magazine, 139-140; involvement in nuclear

power industry, 137, 150; and Joint Committee on Atomic Energy of Congress hearings on fallout, 76-77, 137-138, 141-146; and Joint House-Senate Atomic Radiation Subcommittee hearing, 87; and 1956 move to South Pacific testing ground, 74; opposition to clean bombs, 135; public relations campaign of, for continuance of Plumbbob series, 77-81; report on possible continental testing sites, 29-30; suppression of dissenting scientific views, 36, 80-81, 140-143, 145, 146-150, 153
Atomic Industrial Forum, 150, 153
Atomic power plant, *see* Nuclear power industry
Atomic Tests in Nevada (film), 77
"Atomic Tests in Nevada" (pamphlet), 77-78
"Atoms-for-Peace Plan," Eisenhower's, 136-137
Auxier, John, 122-123, 153

B

Baby Tooth Survey, of St. Louis citizens group, 79
Baldwin, Dr. Bob, 97
Ball, Lt. Col. Frank, 89
Ban, on nuclear testing: Kennedy's plan for official, on atmospheric tests, 140; 1957 unofficial, on atmospheric tests, 136; 1962 official, on atmospheric tests, 141; pressure for, 86-87; Soviet's breaking of unofficial, 138
Bardoli, Martha, 76
Bardoli, Martin (Butch), 76, 79
Battelle Pacific Northwest Labs, 152
Batzel, Dr. Roger, 148
Beebe, Dr. Gilbert, 167
Bergstrom, Jim, 170
Bikini Island: early U.S. atom-bomb tests on, 24, 28; 1956 return of